Table of Contents

Quotes from Federal Employees

"I came to work here because it was a chance to "give back" particularly after 9/11. This was an opportunity to use the skills that I had acquired over 35 years to contribute to our country – really – corny as that sounds. Having been overseas for so long in my previous career, I think I have a unique understanding of how much it means to serve. When you're 8000 miles away the only thing you can really depend upon is the support of our government colleagues working abroad – I wanted to be part of that team – serving in our government."

New Senior Manager from Private Sector

"After my retirement I felt compelled to put my business skills to use in service to my country. The most important factor to me in selecting a civil service job was knowing there would be ample opportunity to leverage my private sector experience in reengineering business processes and developing balanced scorecards."

Retiree from Private Sector

"I had left Federal service in 2000 to pursue private sector professional opportunities. My focus changed a year later, as I started to realize that national needs must come first. In addition, the opportunity to serve at the executive level of Federal service represents a significant professional advancement in my field. I took that opportunity when it became available through an SES candidate development program that was open to non-status candidates. Federal employee benefits for my family were an added incentive. While I took a hit in pay, I decided that making a contribution to public service – and the professional prestige that comes with being a member of the SES – was worth it."

Revolving Employee – SES FED CDP Candidate

"Working with the Federal Government has afforded me the unique privilege of completing my doctorate at GW while also furthering my professional career. Telework, alternative work schedules and a position that has a high-degree of autonomy has provided an effective means of managing a hectic work, life and school balancing act."

Full Time Employee/Graduate Student

Introduction

Federal human capital managers are facing increasing competition in attracting and retaining talented men and women to work in the civilian workforce. To meet this challenge, the Office of Personnel Management (OPM) has developed the Career Patterns initiative – a new approach for bringing the next generation of employees into Federal Government positions. This guide introduces the Career Patterns way of viewing recruiting and presents techniques for identifying opportunities and crafting action plans to ensure employment efforts are successful.

The Changing Environment

The "new normal" for the 21st century workforce will bear little resemblance to that of the late 20th century in which many current Federal managers spent the majority of their careers. This is being exacerbated by several compelling trends that are converging to make immediate planning and action imperative, including:

- A significant retirement wave among current Federal employees is coming – we should expect 40 percent of our workforce to retire between 2006 and 2015.
- Competition for scarce talent among employers throughout the national economy is increasing.
- The applicants we must attract hold differing expectations; their needs and interests have shifted from past generations, which means we must offer a wider variety of employer-employee relationships.

Adopting a 21st Century Mindset

Consider the traditional view of a Federal career – an entry-level employee joins an agency and spends the next 30-plus years coming to work five days a week, in an agency office, on a traditional schedule to provide valuable public service and meet that agency's mission.

That view will continue to describe many positions. However, more and more of the needed and available talent will be interested in something other than this traditional arrangement. To compete successfully for those potential employees, we must adapt to their expectations and create an environment that will support their success. The Federal Government must cultivate, accommodate and advertise the broad range of opportunities and arrangements that will characterize Federal careers in the future. In short, we must develop a new mindset. We are dealing with a 21st century challenge that requires a 21st century approach.

The Career Patterns Approach

Building the environments to attract a wider range of potential employees will require planning and investment in equipment and training. Among other things, we must make sure our managers and leaders have the specific competencies to supervise and manage in nontraditional work settings. That is where the Career Patterns initiative comes in. Using this new approach, Federal human capital managers will be able to shape their workforce planning efforts to build and operate in a broad range of employer-employee arrangements where, for example —

- Retired accountants from private sector firms bring their skills to a Federal agency as a commitment to public service.
- Recent graduates in a specialized environmental management field form a cadre of mobile talent that deploys to wherever the need is greatest.

- Mid-Career technology experts spend a few years on a groundbreaking Federal project before rotating back out to work in the private or non-profit sector.
- Benefits adjudicators review cases and work from home at any hour of the day or night.

Many of the alternative work arrangements that will attract and retain talent are already permissible and in use in many agencies. With a Career Patterns mindset, we will come to think about those different arrangements – telework, flexible work schedules, and varied appointment types – as natural and regular ways of getting work done and not as aberrations.

Getting Started

This guide is your introduction to the Career Patterns initiative and how it can be incorporated into your human capital planning work. Four sections will take you through the process of identifying patterns and hiring attractors for your agency's positions.

- In Section I, you will get an understanding of Career Patterns, their dimensions, and some of the scenarios they generate.
- In Section II, you will learn to use an analytic tool to help you determine your specific hiring requirements and how they can be addressed using the Career Patterns approach.
- In Section III, the two ideas come together so you can build environments in your agency that will produce the greatest benefit from using Career Patterns.
- In Section IV, we provide references and links to the policies and programs that will make Career Patterns work for you.

Ensuring the Federal Government continues to have an effective civilian workforce is an achievable goal. But our success will be greatest if human capital managers throughout Government take a proactive, 21st century approach – the Career Patterns approach – to hiring. This guide will get that process underway.

I. Career Patterns: Dimensions and Scenarios

As a starting point for developing the new mindset a Career Patterns approach to hiring uses, this section provides some Career Patterns basics. A few dimensions for understanding Career Patterns are introduced and discussed briefly. Then those dimensions are applied to create and explore some scenarios where the Career Patterns approach is developed and illustrated further. Terms used throughout the guide are also defined in this section.

Career Pattern Dimensions

OPM's focus on Career Patterns recognizes that employer-employee relationships will increasingly vary across many dimensions. We are considering such determinants as:

- Time in career (early, middle, late, returning annuitants)

- Mobility (among agencies, between public and private sectors)

- Permanence (seasonal/intermittent, long-term, revolving, temporary, students)

- Mission-focus (program-based, project managers)

- Flexible arrangements (detached from office, job sharers, non-traditional time of day, part-time, irregular schedule)

The diagram on the following page illustrates the Career Pattern Dimensions and clarifies them further. These dimensions offer insights to both individuals and to work situations. Each employee – or potential employee – can be characterized by identifying the point on each dimension that best matches his or her description or interests. Similarly, each civil service position can be categorized by identifying the range along each dimension that could characterize an effective working arrangement for an employee who fills the position.

Career Patterns Dimensions

Time in Career

The career stage at which one enters or re-enters the Federal workforce, i.e., student workers, interns, mid or late career individuals, or retirees.

Early————————————————►Middle————————————————►Late/Returning

A work environment that welcomes entry at different stages of career from novice to retiree

Mobility

The movement of an employee, i.e., geographic location changes, changing between agencies, the public and private sectors, movement upward or across career paths

Not Mobile◄————————————————►Mobile◄————————————————►Highly Mobile

A work environment that welcomes advancement within and across occupations, organizations, and sectors

Permanence

The duration of employment that suits the employee and the mission, i.e., seasonal/intermittent, temporary, long term, revolving

Short Term◄————————————————►Revolving◄————————————————►Long Term

A work environment that welcomes those who want to work temporarily, occasionally, or indefinitely

Mission-Focus

The mission or project that attracts one to Federal employment, i.e., public service generally, a profession of choice in any agency, or seeking the program or project specific to one agency

Public Service Driven◄————————►Profession Driven◄————————►Specific Mission Driven

A work environment that welcomes all motivations, from general service commitment to a specific passion

Flexible Arrangements

The work environment that best supports the employee and the work, i.e., telework, non-traditional hours, job sharing, expanded benefits, physical workspace and infrastructure, and work structure

Traditional◄————————————————►Flexible◄————————————————►Highly Flexible

A work environment that welcomes and accommodates traditional and flexible work arrangements

◄————————————————Dimension Spectrum————————————————►

United States Office of Personnel Management

Career Pattern Scenarios

Through research[1] and discussion, we have applied the Career Pattern Dimensions and identified Career Pattern Scenarios that describe the particular characteristics of ten types of individuals who could help broaden the pool of potential employees for Federal Government jobs. These ten Career Pattern Scenarios are good starting points for attracting additional employees to the Federal civilian workforce. However, the ten scenarios we explore in depth in this guide are by no means exhaustive, and we encourage agencies to develop and use their own Career Pattern Scenarios.

Each of the ten Career Pattern Scenarios we identified is related principally, but not exclusively, to one of the Career Pattern Dimensions, as shown below.

Dimensions	Scenarios
Time in Career	• Student • New Professional* • Mid-Career Professional* • Retiree
Mobility	• Highly Mobile
Permanence	• Revolving • Term
Mission-Focus	• Mission-Focused • Experienced Professional* (specific fields)
Flexible Arrangements	• Requires Flexibilities

* In these scenarios, the term "Professional" is used to denote applicant experience, rather than its specialized Federal HR meaning, i.e., an occupation that has a positive education requirement.

[1] See bibliography in Appendix B

Definitions

This guide introduces a number of terms and concepts that may be new to the user. The following definitions will help orient the user to the language used throughout the guide.

- <u>Job requirements</u> are the specific, definable requirements that reflect the employment needs in your agency. Identified through strategic workforce planning and analysis, they are best understood as the end objectives of your workforce planning efforts – what you are trying to accomplish in terms of the numbers, occupations and other characteristics of employees you seek to hire and retain. As a whole, they represent the workforce for which you will need to build an appealing work environment.

- <u>Work environment</u> refers to the qualities and characteristics of the experience of working in your agency. Put simply, it is an expression of what it is like to work in your organization – the employer-employee relationships and work setting. Understanding which aspects of your work environment appeal to applicants and which do not can help you prioritize work environment changes.

- A <u>Career Pattern Scenario</u> is a configuration of values across five Career Pattern Dimensions. As such, each particular scenario characterizes a segment of the general labor market that has similar expectations for the kind of work environment that is appealing. This guide explores ten distinct Career Pattern Scenarios: Student, New Professional, Mid-Career Professional, Retiree, Highly Mobile, Revolving, Term, Mission-Focused, Experienced Professional, and Requires Flexibilities.

- <u>Career Pattern Dimensions</u> are key aspects of the work environment that must be understood and shaped in order to appeal to workers in a particular Career Pattern Scenario. The Career Patterns initiative uses the five dimensions shown on page 4.

- <u>Categorization</u> refers to the process and outcome of matching particular job requirements with one or more Career Pattern Scenarios. It is a first step toward the goal of building desirable and effective work environments.

- <u>Core Values</u> are the fundamental beliefs, interests, demands and concerns that individuals hold. Research indicates particular constellations of these core values are associated with various Career Pattern Scenarios. Keeping these values in mind when appealing to potential employees from a particular scenario can effectively focus recruitment efforts.

- <u>Work Attractors</u> are those features of employer-employee relationships and work arrangements that engage interest and commitment from job applicants and employees, in part based on their significance for related core values. Providing information about work attractors is essential for effectively recruiting across Career Pattern Scenarios and Dimensions.

An Initial Set of Career Pattern Scenarios

In the following diagrams and descriptions of Career Pattern Scenarios, we identify where typical individuals who fit the Career Pattern Scenario would be placed along each of the five Career Pattern Dimensions. For each scenario, we also present:

- the core values and work attractors for typical potential employees who fit the scenario
- relevant human resources management policies and practices that are particularly promising for that scenario, and
- considerations for attracting and retaining potential employees under the scenario.

The next 20 pages are to be viewed in pairs. One such pair of pages from the ten sets that follow is shown in miniature below. The left-hand page provides a quick view of a Career Pattern Scenario by showing the location on each Career Pattern Dimension that characterizes a typical individual who fits that scenario. It also presents a brief description of the scenario. The right-hand page presents Core Values, Work Attractors, Human Resources Policies/Programs To Leverage, and considerations to Support Recruitment and Retention under that scenario.

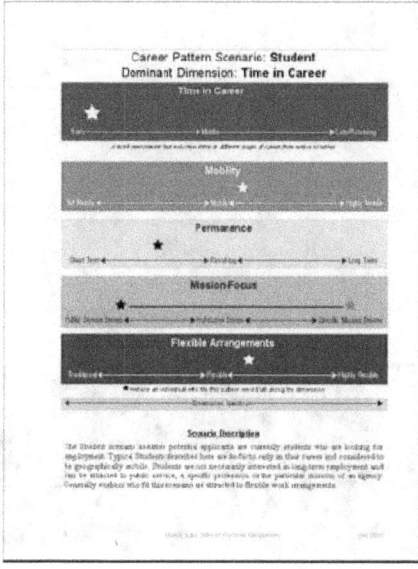

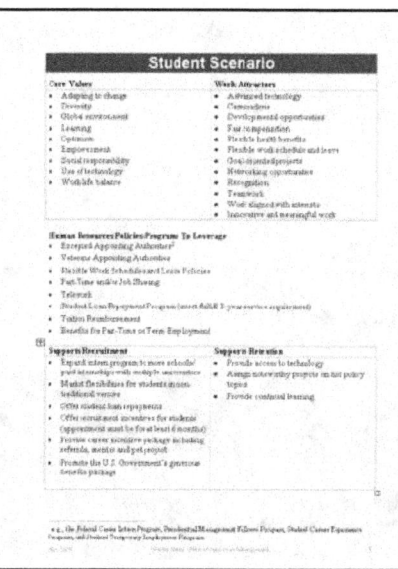

Career Pattern Scenario: **Student**
Dominant Dimension: **Time in Career**

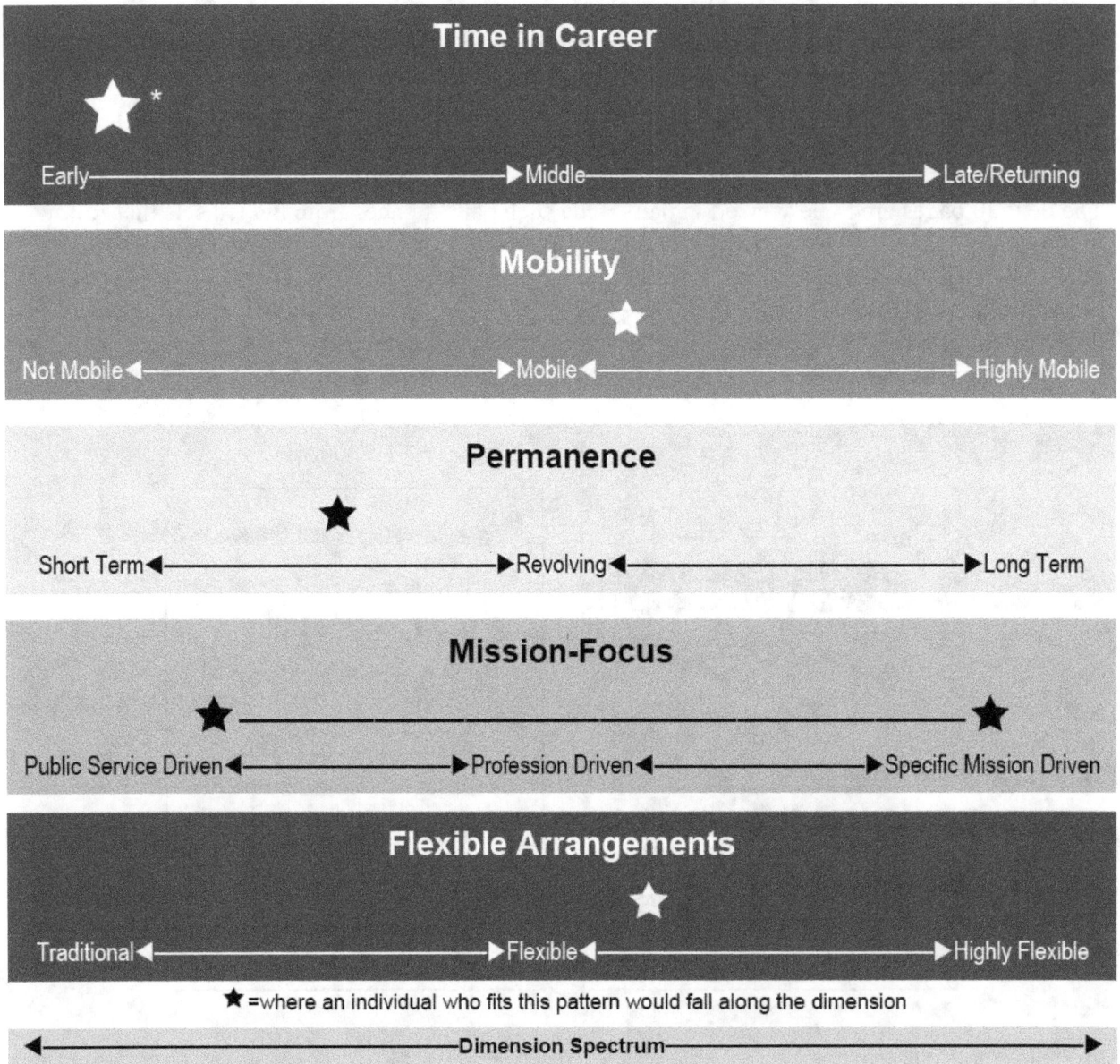

* In each Career Pattern Scenario diagram, the star that appears in the dominant dimension, e.g., Time in Career for Student, is larger than stars in the remaining dimensions.

Scenario Description

The Student scenario assumes potential applicants are currently students who are looking for employment. Typical Students described here are de-facto early in their career and considered to be geographically mobile. Students are not necessarily interested in long-term employment and can be attracted to public service, a specific profession or the particular mission of an agency. Generally workers who fit this scenario are attracted to flexible work arrangements.

Student Scenario

Core Values
- Adapting to change
- Diversity
- Global environment
- Learning
- Optimism
- Empowerment
- Social responsibility
- Use of technology
- Work-life balance

Work Attractors
- Advanced technology
- Camaraderie
- Developmental opportunities
- Fair compensation
- Flexible health benefits
- Flexible work schedule and leave
- Goal-oriented projects
- Networking opportunities
- Recognition
- Teamwork
- Work aligned with interests
- Innovative and meaningful work

Human Resources Policies/Programs To Leverage
- Excepted Appointing Authorities[2]
- Veterans Appointing Authorities
- Flexible Work Schedules and Leave Policies
- Part-Time and/or Job Sharing
- Telework
- Student Loan Repayment Program (must fulfill 3-year service requirement)
- Tuition Reimbursement
- Temporary Limited, Term, and Other Than Full-time Career Employment

Supports Recruitment
- Expand intern program to more schools/ paid internships with multiple universities
- Market flexibilities for students in non-traditional venues
- Offer student loan repayments
- Offer recruitment incentives for students (appointment must be for at least 6 months)
- Provide career incentive package including referrals, mentor and pet project
- Promote the U.S. Government's generous benefits package

Supports Retention
- Provide access to technology
- Assign noteworthy projects on hot policy topics
- Provide continual learning

---

[2] e.g., the Federal Career Intern Program, Presidential Management Fellows Program, Student Career Experience Program, and Student Temporary Employment Program

Career Pattern Scenario: **New Professional**
Dominant Dimension: **Time in Career**

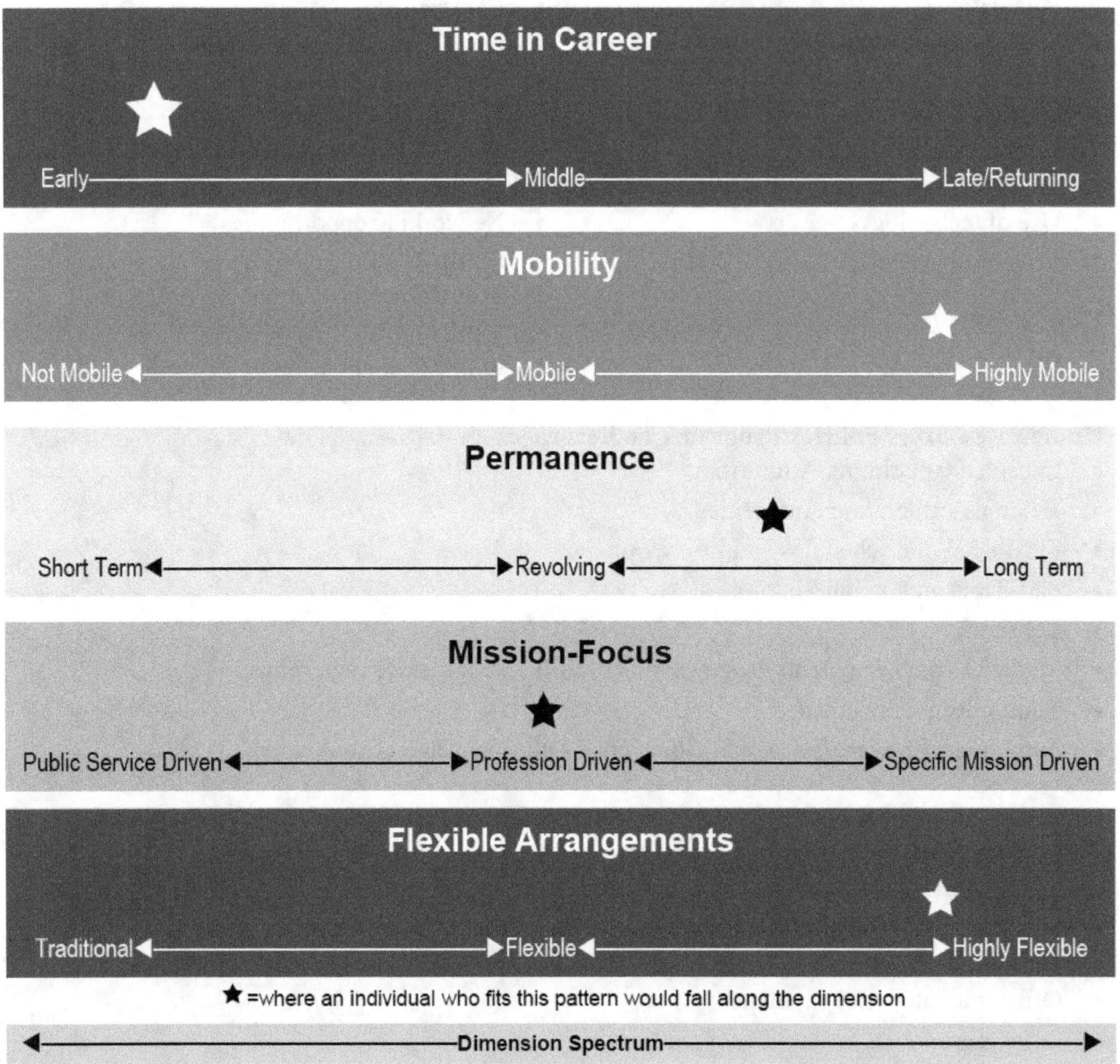

Time in Career
Early————————————▶Middle————————————▶Late/Returning

Mobility
Not Mobile◀————————————▶Mobile◀————————————▶Highly Mobile

Permanence
Short Term◀————————————▶Revolving◀————————————▶Long Term

Mission-Focus
Public Service Driven◀————————————▶Profession Driven◀————————————▶Specific Mission Driven

Flexible Arrangements
Traditional◀————————————▶Flexible◀————————————▶Highly Flexible

★ =where an individual who fits this pattern would fall along the dimension

◀————————————Dimension Spectrum————————————▶

Scenario Description

Typical New Professionals are embarking on a new career and have less than 5 years experience in the workforce. They are college graduates who are not bound to a specific geographic location, but do seek a somewhat permanent position. While they may still be developing within their profession or desired job function, they are very attracted to work in their areas of interest. New Professional applicants are looking for a work environment that offers the most flexible arrangements.

New Professional Scenario

Core Values
- Diversity
- Adapting to change
- Confidence and self-reliance
- Innovation and creativity
- Non-traditional workplace
- Social responsibility
- Work-life balance

Work Attractors
- Advanced technology
- Camaraderie
- Developmental opportunities
- Competitive compensation
- Flexible health benefits
- Flexible work schedule and leave
- Goal-oriented projects
- Networking opportunities
- Recognition
- Teamwork
- Innovative work aligned with interests

Human Resources Policies/Programs To Leverage
- Recruitment and/or Relocation Incentives
- Superior Qualifications and Special Needs Pay-Setting Authority
- Term Appointment
- Excepted Appointing Authorities[3]
- Veterans Appointing Authorities
- Direct Hire Authority (pursuant to regulatory requirements)
- Flexible Work Schedules and Leave Policies
- Student Loan Repayment Program (must fulfill 3-year service requirement)
- Tuition Reimbursement and TSP Matching Contribution Paid by the Government
- Telework
- Flexible Spending Accounts
- Childcare and Eldercare Benefits

Supports Recruitment
- Hire with a quick and transparent process
- Market through professional associations and employ other innovative marketing
- Offer recruitment incentives
- Offer student loan repayments and tuition reimbursement for further education
- Promote the U.S. Government's generous benefits package
- Promote TSP matching contributions and rollover

Supports Retention
- Assign a variety of projects related to service
- Create a career ladder with noncompetitive promotion opportunities
- Offer professional development opportunities
- Offer salaries competitive with private sector to the extent possible
- Recognize and reward creativity and performance

---

[3] e.g., the Federal Career Intern Program, Presidential Management Fellows Program, and Student Career Experience Program

Career Pattern Scenario: **Mid-Career Professional**
Dominant Dimension: **Time in Career**

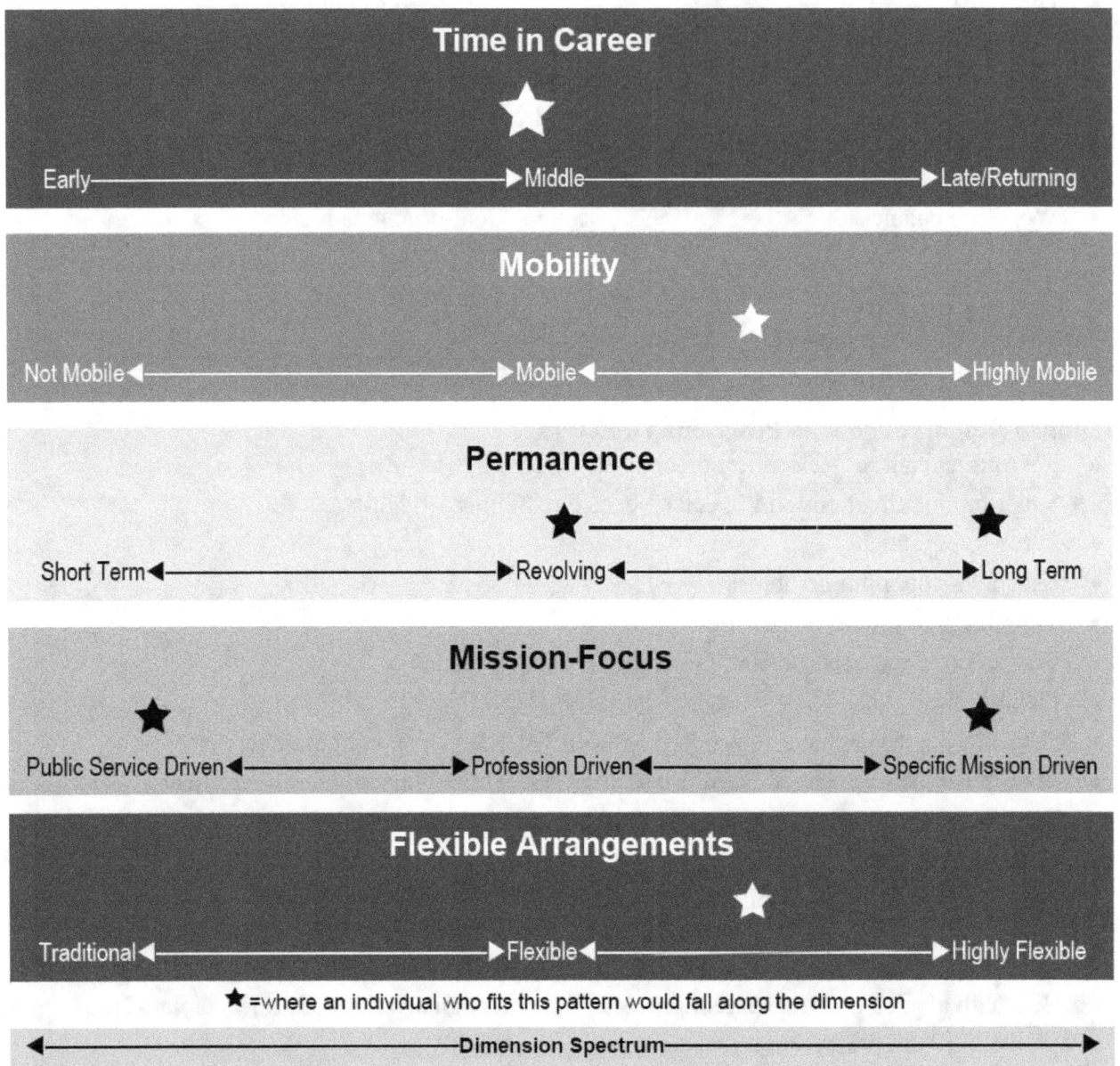

★ =where an individual who fits this pattern would fall along the dimension

◄————————————————Dimension Spectrum————————————————►

Scenario Description

Mid-Career Professionals have more than 10 years work experience and are looking for opportunities that will capitalize on their expertise. They are not uncomfortable moving from one employer to another, but may well be attracted to long-term employment if the work allows for innovation and creativity. Mid-Career Professional applicants tend to need more flexible arrangements to create work-life balance and can be attracted to the idea of serving the public or to a specific agency mission. These potential applicants may also look to rotate in and out of the public sector or between agencies to work on specific projects.

Mid-Career Professional Scenario

Core Values
- Diversity
- Adapting to change
- Innovation and creativity
- Efficiency
- Professionalism
- Work-life balance

Work Attractors
- Developmental opportunities
- Competitive compensation
- Flexible health benefits
- Flexible work schedule and leave
- Networking opportunities
- Recognition
- Retirement benefits
- Teamwork
- Technical and logistical support

Human Resources Policies/Programs To Leverage
- Excepted Service Appointing Authorities[4]
- Veterans Appointing Authorities
- Expert and Consultant Appointing Authority
- Part-time and/or Job Sharing
- Recruitment and/ or Relocation Incentives
- Superior Qualifications and Special Needs Pay-Setting Authority
- Flexible Work Schedules and Leave Policies
- Telework

Supports Recruitment
- Promote the U.S. Government's generous benefits package
- Hire with a quick and transparent process
- Open more mid-career vacancies to competition from external applicants
- Market to target audiences and promote positive aspects of public service

Supports Retention
- Create opportunities to use and build skills
- Offer professional development opportunities
- Offer salaries competitive with the private and non-profit sectors to the extent possible

---

[4] e.g., the Senior Presidential Management Fellows Program

Career Pattern Scenario: **Retiree**
Dominant Dimension: **Time in Career**

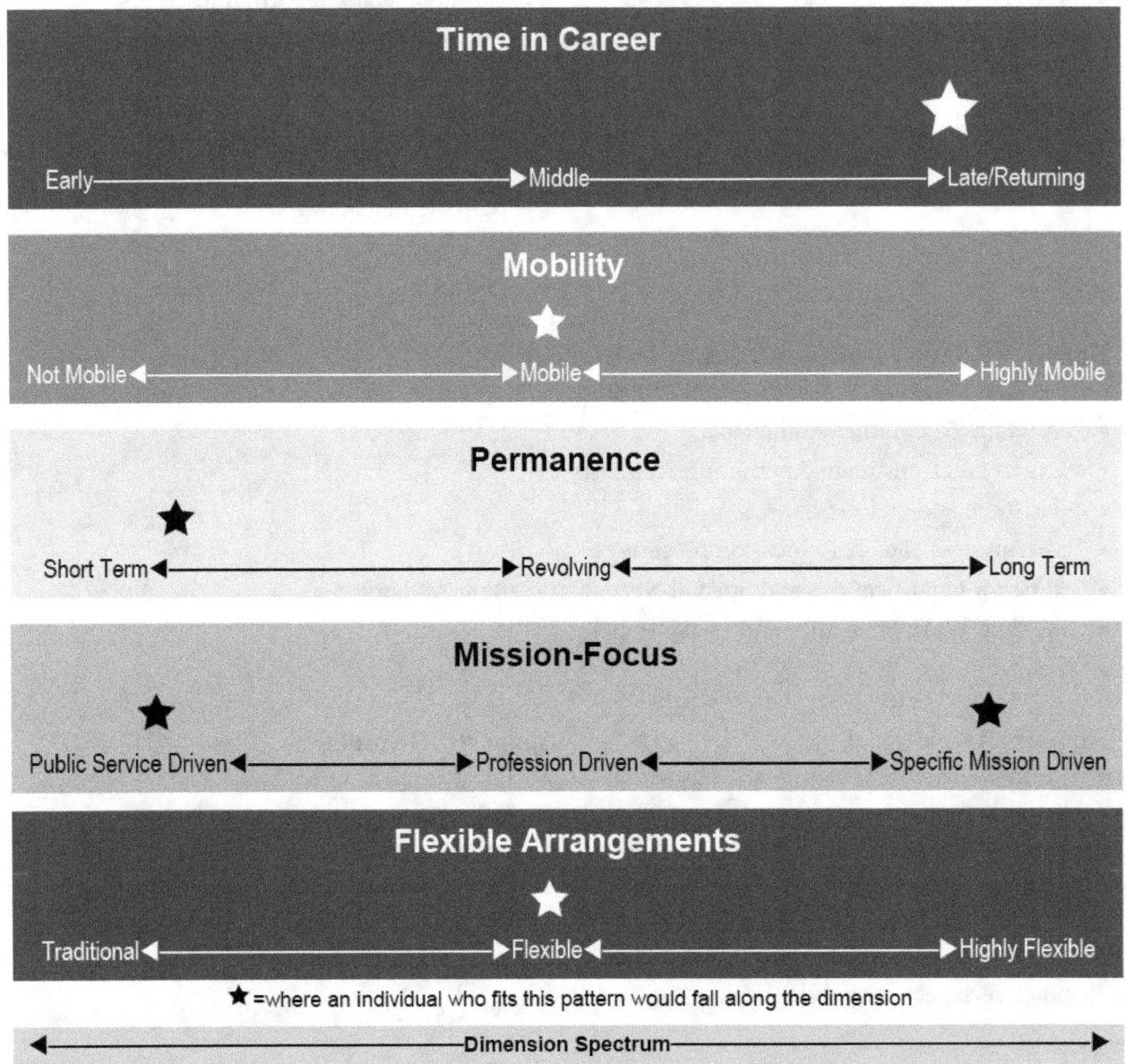

Scenario Description

Within this scenario, Retirees are people who have retired from careers inside or outside Federal service, possess valuable skills and competencies, and are interested in working for the Government either in a full-time or part-time capacity. Retiree applicants tend to be mobile across agencies. They may require more flexible work arrangements to accommodate their schedules and desired work location.

Retiree Scenario

Core Values
- Security for a better future
- Deference to authority
- Good work ethic
- Loyalty
- Persistence
- Self-sacrifice and deferral of rewards
- Work-life balance

Work Attractors
- Camaraderie
- Fair compensation
- Flexible work schedule and leave
- Work aligned with interests
- Innovative and meaningful work
- Teamwork

Human Resources Policies/Programs To Leverage
- Reinstatement Eligibility (if applicable)
- Superior Qualifications and Special Needs Pay-Setting Authority
- Flexible Work Schedules and Leave Policies
- Part-time and/ or Job Sharing
- Expert and Consultant Appointing Authority
- Maximum Payable Rate Rule (highest previous rate)
- Recruitment and/or Relocation Incentives
- Telework
- Temporary and Term Appointments
- Eldercare Benefits
- TSP Matching Contribution Paid by the Government
- Benefits for Part-Time, Temporary Limited, Seasonal, or Intermittent

Supports Recruitment
- Create part-time and flexible work options
- Deploy experts to recruit experts
- Market the mission
- Market work-related training

Supports Retention
- Assign meaningful projects
- Offer opportunities to mentor others
- Ensure open, direct communications
- Offer stress reduction programs

Career Pattern Scenario: **Highly Mobile**
Dominant Dimension: **Mobility**

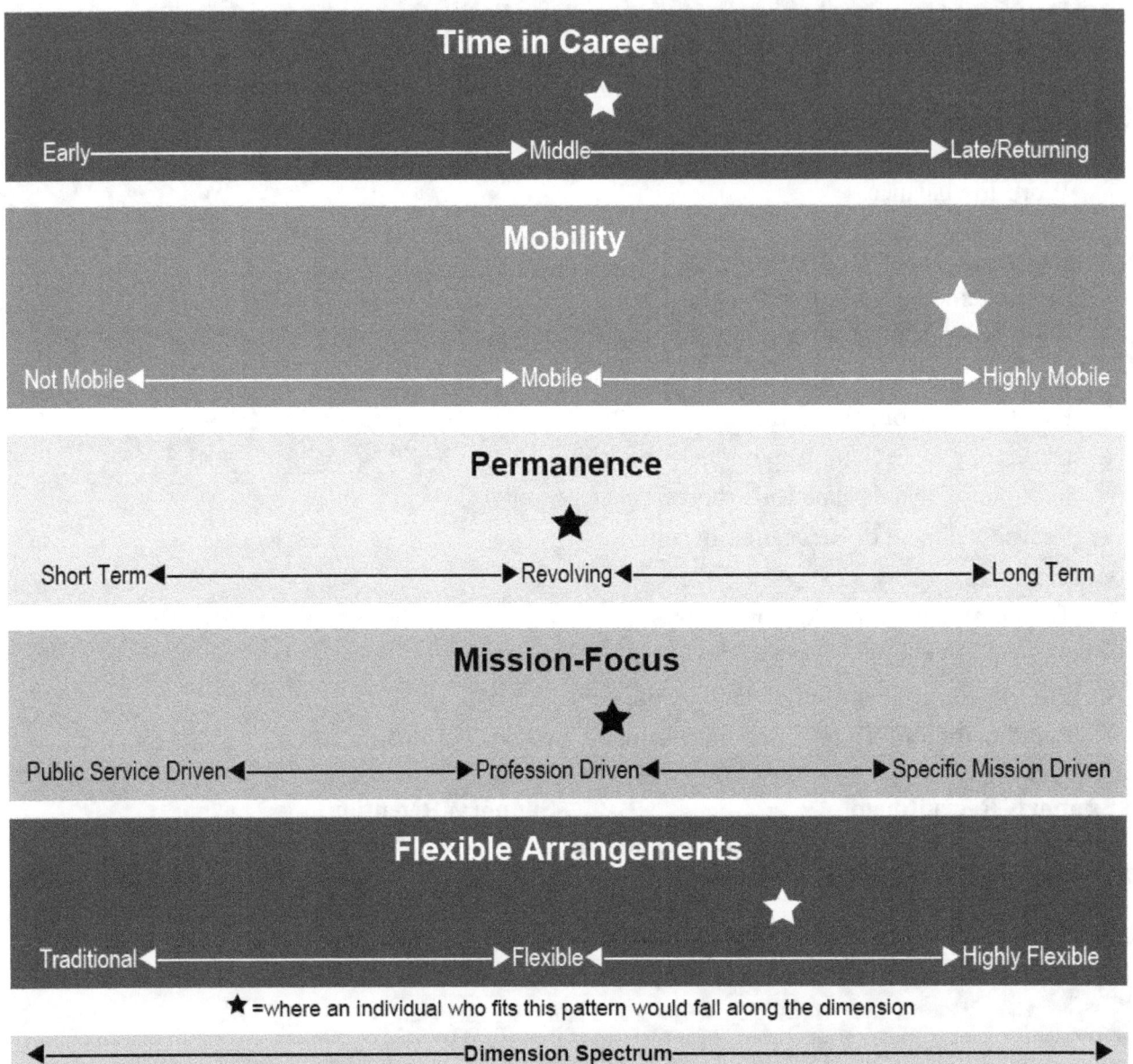

★ =where an individual who fits this pattern would fall along the dimension

◄────────────────Dimension Spectrum────────────────►

Scenario Description

The Highly Mobile scenario describes people who desire mobility either geographically or, once hired, between agencies. Typical Highly Mobile applicants require flexibilities in their work arrangements to accommodate their movement. These individuals will look for the best opportunity to do the work they love.

Highly Mobile Scenario

Core Values
- Constant learning
- Independence
- Optimism
- Self-motivation

Work Attractors
- Advanced technology
- Benefits portability
- Developmental opportunities
- Fair compensation
- Flexible health benefits
- Flexible work schedule and leave
- Goal-oriented projects
- Networking opportunities
- Technical, administrative and logistical support
- Work aligned with interests
- Innovative and meaningful work

Human Resources Policies/Programs To Leverage
- Appointment of Expert and Consultants
- Flexible Work Schedules and Leave Policies
- Part-time and/or Job Sharing
- Maximum Payable Rate Rule (highest previous rate)
- Reinstatement Eligibility
- Recruitment and/ or Relocation Incentives
- Student Loan Repayment Program (must fulfill 3-year service requirement)
- Superior Qualifications and Special Needs Pay-Setting Authority
- Telework
- Temporary and Term Appointments
- Veterans Appointing Authorities
- TSP Matching Contribution Paid by the Government

Supports Recruitment
- Create part-time and flexible work options
- Deploy experts to recruit experts
- Promote the U.S. Government's generous and portable benefits package
- Market the mission
- Market work-related training

Supports Retention
- Offer professional development opportunities
- Work to increase employee engagement, particularly among new employees
- Provide relocation support
- Reward and recognize contributions

Career Pattern Scenario: **Revolving**
Dominant Dimension: **Permanence**

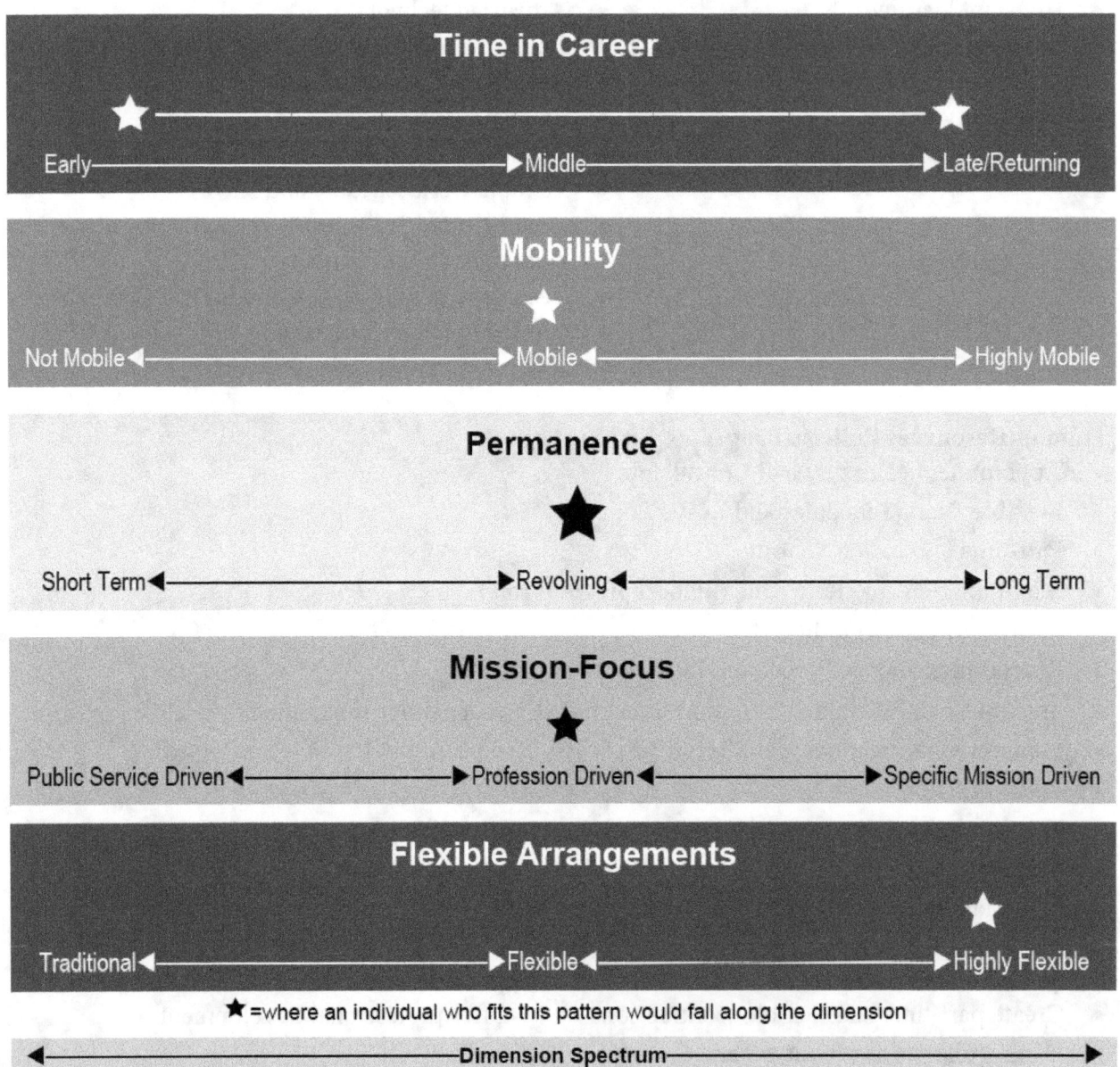

Time in Career

Early————————————————▶Middle————————————————▶Late/Returning

Mobility

Not Mobile◀————————————————▶Mobile◀————————————————▶Highly Mobile

Permanence

Short Term◀————————————————▶Revolving◀————————————————▶Long Term

Mission-Focus

Public Service Driven◀————————————————▶Profession Driven◀————————————————▶Specific Mission Driven

Flexible Arrangements

Traditional◀————————————————▶Flexible◀————————————————▶Highly Flexible

★ =where an individual who fits this pattern would fall along the dimension

◀————————————————Dimension Spectrum————————————————▶

Scenario Description

Typical applicants in the Revolving scenario are those individuals who, at any stage of their career, are looking to maximize their opportunities by moving in and out of Federal service. They tend to require flexible hours and portable benefits. Revolving applicants may look for seasonal or intermittent work that supports their profession or job interests.

Revolving Scenario

Core Values
- Adapting to change
- Confidence and self-reliance
- Recognition
- Use of technology
- Constant learning
- Diversity
- Good work ethic
- Work-life balance

Work Attractors
- Portable benefits
- Developmental opportunities
- Fair compensation
- Flexible work schedule and leave
- Goal-oriented projects
- Networking opportunities
- Recognition
- Meaningful work

Human Resources Policies/Programs To Leverage
- Appointment of Expert and Consultants
- Excepted Appointing Authorities[5]
- Flexible Work Schedules and Leave Policies
- Intergovernmental Personnel Act (IPA) Mobility Program
- Maximum Payable Rate Rule (highest previous rate)
- Reinstatement Eligibility
- Recruitment and/or Relocation Incentives
- Superior Qualifications and Special Needs Pay-Setting Authority
- Telework
- Temporary and Term Appointments

Supports Recruitment
- Develop recruiting outreach programs in professional organizations
- Promote the U.S. Government's generous benefits package
- Market interesting and challenging work
- Recognize value of non-Federal work
- Speed recruitment process

Supports Retention
- Establish a system for maintaining contact with employees and who leave the agency (other than for cause)
- Make the hiring process transparent
- Offer opportunities for learning and rotations
- Provide challenging work
- Provide variety in work assignments
- Recognize contributions

---

[5] e.g., the Federal Career Intern Program and Presidential Management Fellows Program

Career Pattern Scenario: **Term**
Dominant Dimension: **Permanence**

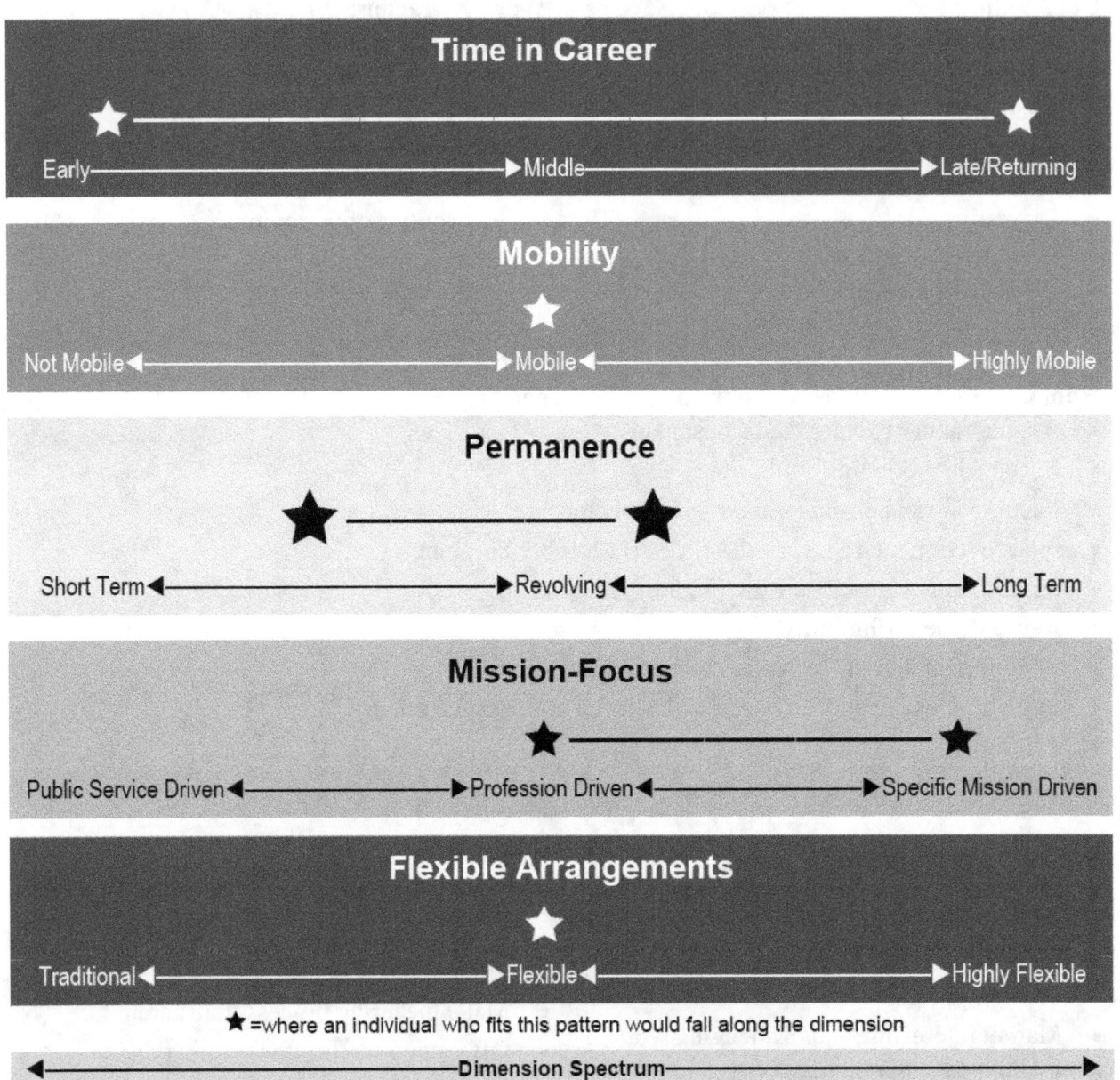

Time in Career

Early————————————▶Middle————————————▶Late/Returning

Mobility

Not Mobile◀————————————▶Mobile◀————————————▶Highly Mobile

Permanence

Short Term◀————————————▶Revolving◀————————————▶Long Term

Mission-Focus

Public Service Driven◀————————————▶Profession Driven◀————————————▶Specific Mission Driven

Flexible Arrangements

Traditional◀————————————▶Flexible◀————————————▶Highly Flexible

★ =where an individual who fits this pattern would fall along the dimension

◀————————————Dimension Spectrum————————————▶

Scenario Description

Typical applicants under the Term scenario are those who seek to hold a position in the Government for a specific responsibility over a short period of time (no more than 4 years). These people are driven by their professional interests. They require a work environment that supports short term work and has portable benefits and flexible options for location and work structure.

Term Scenario

Core Values
- Use of technology
- Recognition
- Diversity
- Good work ethic
- Work-life balance

Work Attractors
- Portable benefits
- Goal-oriented projects
- Competitive compensation

Human Resources Policies/Programs To Leverage
- Temporary and Term Appointments
- Excepted Appointing Authorities[6]
- Flexible Work Schedules and Leave Flexibilities
- Intergovernmental Personnel Act (IPA) Mobility Program
- Reinstatement Eligibility (if applicable)
- Superior Qualifications and Special Needs Pay-Setting Authority
- Temporary Limited, Term, and Other than Full-time Career Employment

Supports Recruitment
- Develop recruiting outreach programs in professional organizations
- Promote the U.S. Government's generous benefits package
- Include specific projects in announcement
- Recognize value of non-Federal work
- Use hiring flexibilities

Supports Retention
- Help employee maintain work/life balance
- Recognize contributions

---

[6] e.g., the Federal Career Intern Program and Student Career Experience Program

Career Pattern Scenario: **Mission-Focused**
Dominant Dimension: **Mission-Focus**

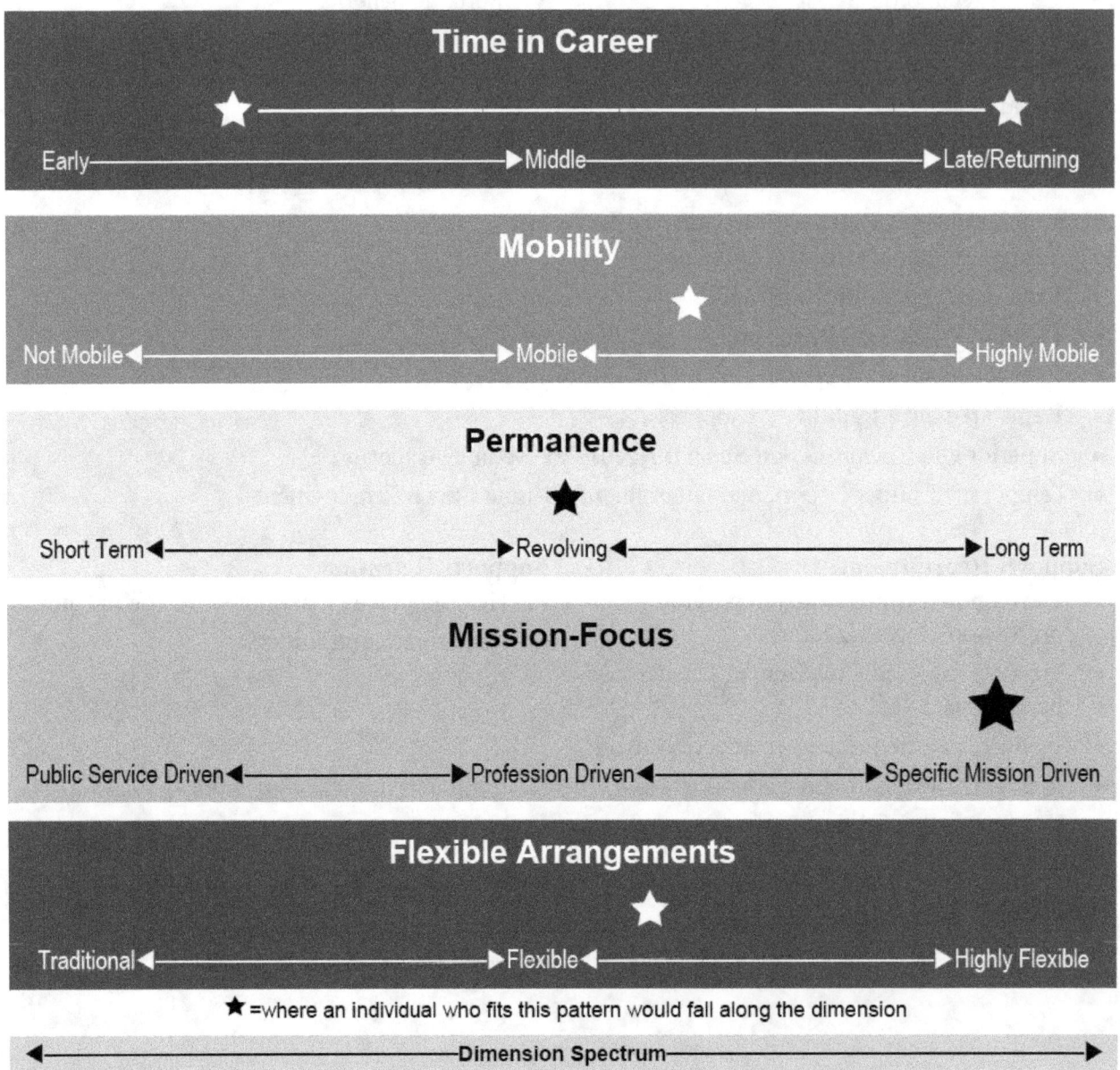

Scenario Description

Typical Mission-Focused applicants are drawn to Federal service to support a specific agency mission. Knowing they can make a contribution and be recognized for that contribution is a critical work environment requirement for Mission-Focused potential applicants. Individuals under this scenario can be at almost any stage in their career.

Mission-Focused Scenario

Core Values
- Knowledge
- Passion for subject, interest, or service
- Work related to expertise/interests
- Social responsibility

Work Attractors
- Camaraderie
- Developmental opportunities
- Goal-oriented projects
- Research environment and freedom
- Teamwork
- Work aligned with interests
- Meaningful work

Human Resources Policies/Programs To Leverage
- Direct Hire Authority
- Excepted Service Appointed Authorities[7]
- Recruitment and/or Relocation Incentives
- Student Loan Repayment Program (must fulfill 3-year service requirement)
- Maximum Payable Rate Rule (highest previous rate)
- Superior Qualifications and Special Needs Pay-Setting Authority
- Telework
- Veterans Appointing Authorities

Supports Recruitment
- Advertise the position's link to agency mission
- Market at schools or through specific venues
- Recruit through professional associations and reputable societies
- Time recruitment to parallel current events that inspire service

Supports Retention
- Allow for a variety of projects related to service
- Assistance in maintaining licenses
- Offer professional development opportunities
- Offer salaries competitive with private sector to the extent possible
- Provide dual career ladders

---

[7] e.g., the Federal Career Intern Program

Career Pattern Scenario: **Experienced Professional**
(specific fields)
Dominant Dimension: **Mission-Focus**

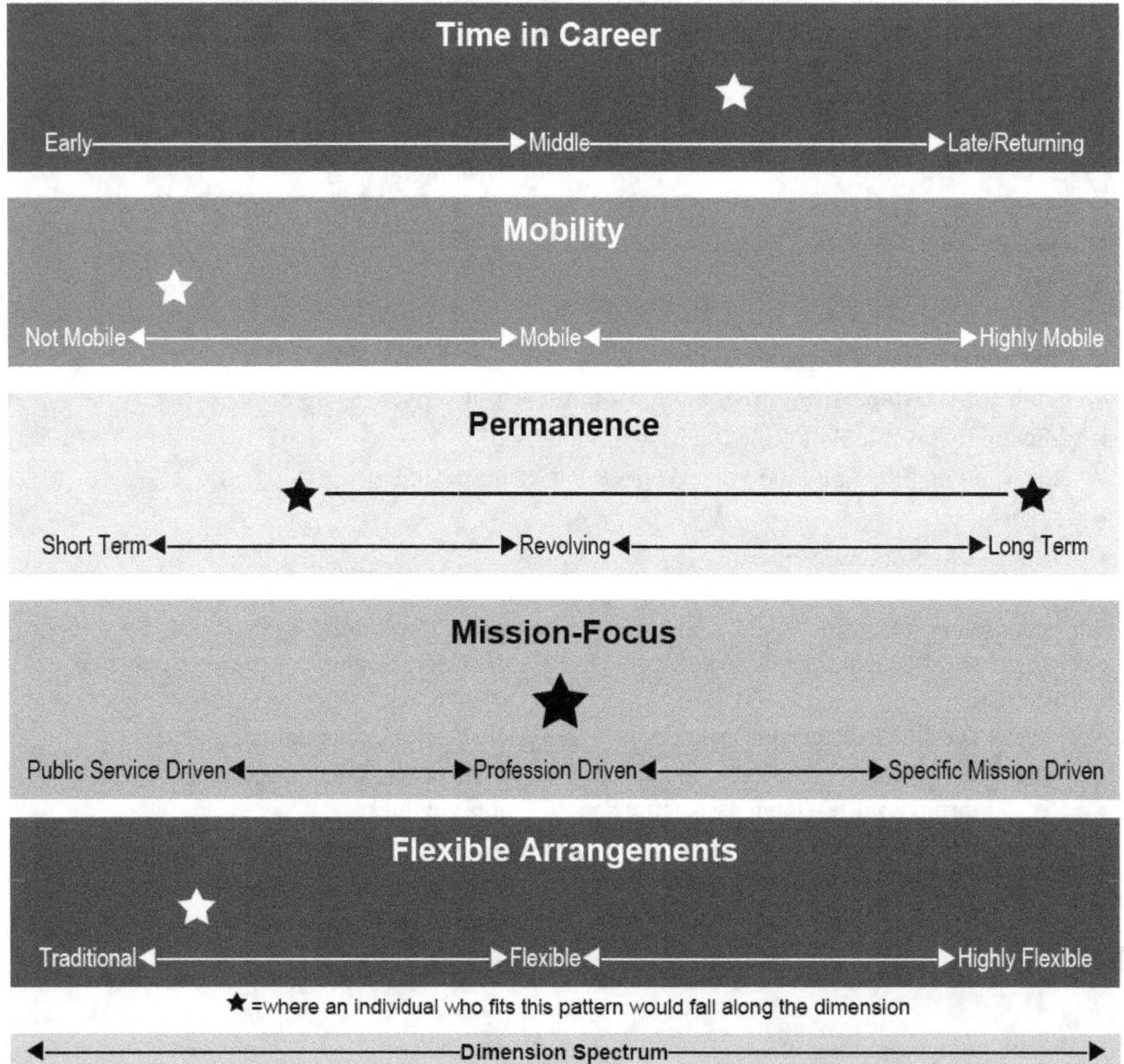

★ =where an individual who fits this pattern would fall along the dimension

←————————————Dimension Spectrum————————————→

Scenario Description

Typical Experienced Professionals are individuals who have a great deal of experience in a specific field (e.g., doctor, accountant, engineer, etc.). With an advanced degrees or certification required for specialized employment, Experienced Professional potential applicants may be interested in a short-term project or a permanent position and seek to make a strong contribution in their area of expertise.

Experienced Professional Scenario
(specific fields)

Core Values
- Commitment to specific field or subject area
- Optimism
- Skills of profession
- Work-life balance

Work Attractors
- Camaraderie
- Fair compensation
- Flexible work schedule and leave
- Recognition
- Teamwork
- Technical and logistical support
- Work aligned with interests
- Innovative and meaningful work

Human Resources Policies/Programs To Leverage
- Flexible Work Schedules and Leave Policies
- Retention and/or Relocation Incentives
- Expert and Consultant Appointing Authority
- Veterans Appointing Authorities
- Superior Qualifications and Special Needs Pay-Setting Authority
- Maximum Payable Rate Rule (highest previous rate)
- Telework
- Childcare and Eldercare Benefits

Supports Recruitment
- Create unique projects for which they can apply skills and expertise
- Involve them in becoming a mentor or subject matter expert
- Offer recruitment incentives
- Recruit through professional associations

Supports Retention
- Offer professional development opportunities
- Offer salaries competitive with private and non-profit sector to the extent possible
- Offer opportunities to mentor others
- Reward and recognize for contributions
- Support networking and professional involvement

Career Pattern Scenario: **Requires Flexibilities**
Dominant Dimension: **Flexible Arrangements**

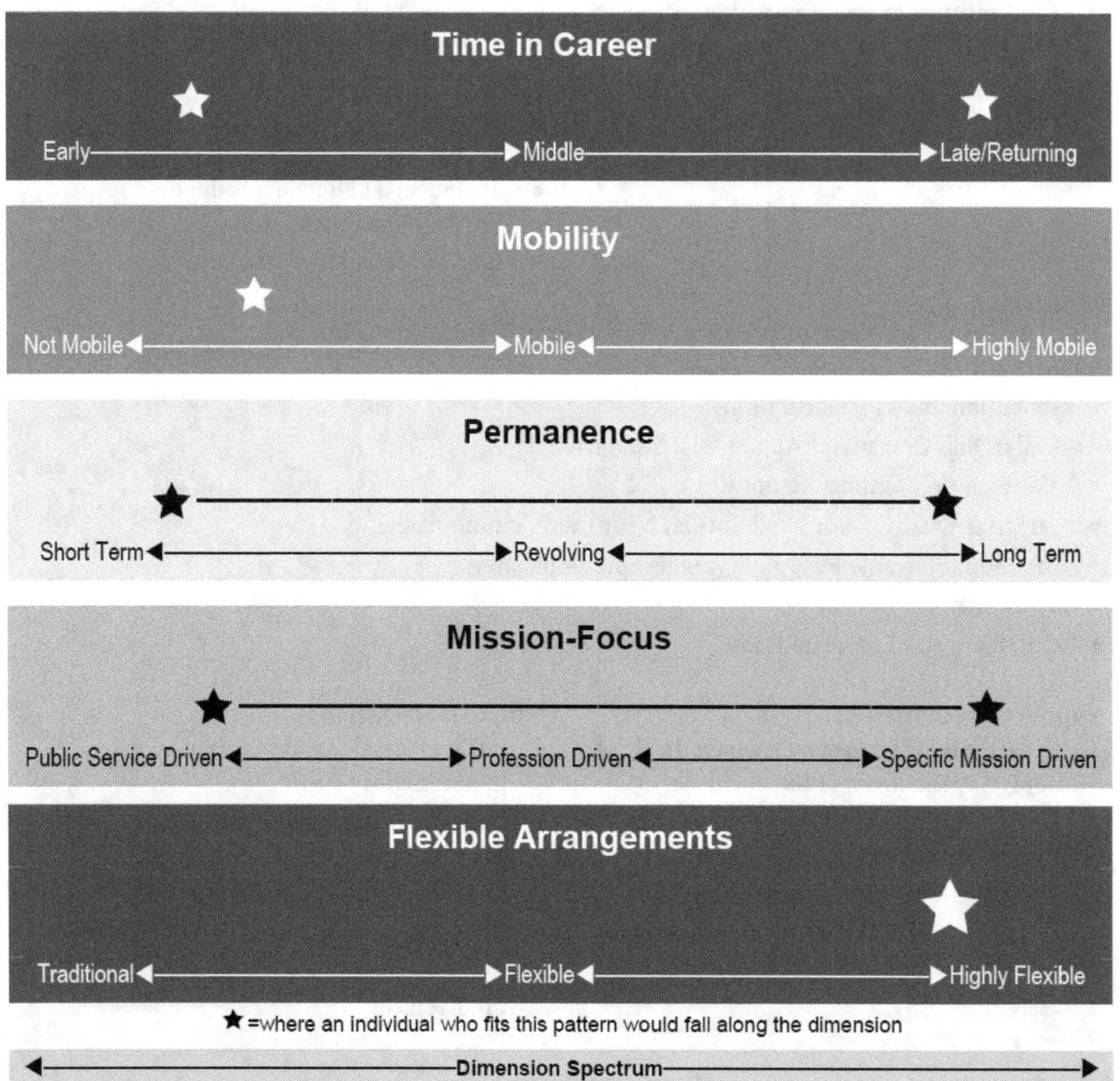

Time in Career
Early—————————————————▶Middle—————————————————▶Late/Returning

Mobility
Not Mobile◀—————————————————▶Mobile◀—————————————————▶Highly Mobile

Permanence
Short Term◀—————————————————▶Revolving◀—————————————————▶Long Term

Mission-Focus
Public Service Driven◀—————————————————▶Profession Driven◀—————————————————▶Specific Mission Driven

Flexible Arrangements
Traditional◀—————————————————▶Flexible◀—————————————————▶Highly Flexible

★ =where an individual who fits this pattern would fall along the dimension

◀—————————————————Dimension Spectrum—————————————————▶

Scenario Description

The Requires Flexibilities scenario describes applicants who are looking for a high level of flexibility in hours, leave, work location and/ or work structure. The applicants' needs may be as range from working at home during non-traditional hours to job sharing in order to manage childcare or eldercare needs. Although typical Requires Flexibilities applicants are not particularly mobile, they may be working at any point in their career and can be interested in any type of work.

Requires Flexibilities Scenario

Core Values
- Mobility
- Family and personal health
- Work-life balance

Work Attractors
- Advanced technology
- Flexible health benefits
- Flexible work schedule and leave
- Technical and logistical support

Human Resources Policies/Programs To Leverage
- Childcare and Eldercare Benefits
- Excepted Service Appointing Authorities[8]
- Flexible Spending Accounts
- Flexible Work Schedules and Leave Policies
- Part-time and/or Job Sharing
- Telework
- Benefits for Part-Time, Temporary Limited, Seasonal, or Intermittent

Supports Recruitment
- Support telework
- Offer recruitment incentives
- Publicize success stories of other employees using flexible arrangements
- Use non-traditional recruiting techniques (e.g., attend night job fairs, host online recruiting fairs with messaging capabilities)
- Structure job to require less in-person interaction

Supports Retention
- Enable a high degree of independent work
- Extend mentor and Subject Matter Expert (SME) programs to employees using flexible arrangements
- Offer professional development opportunities
- Reward and recognize contributions
- Work to increase employee engagement, particularly among those working out of the office

---

[8] e.g., the Student Career Experience Program

II. Career Patterns Analytic Tool

This section provides an analytic tool for using the Career Patterns approach. The tool consists of a structured process with associated worksheets that will help agencies analyze job requirements and produce an evidence-based foundation for building effective work environments. Those reshaped work environments will offer features consistent with future employees' different expectations of the employer-employee relationship and appeal to the multi-dimensional 21st century workforce. In particular, the Career Patterns Analytic Tool lets agencies identify and categorize their job requirements according to Career Pattern Scenarios.

Strategic Workforce Planning and the Analytic Tool

The analysis process described in this section and strategic workforce planning are mutually reinforcing. Applying the analytic tool focuses agencies' strategic workforce planning efforts; and future workforce planning efforts will benefit from the input provided by the Career Patterns analysis. However, applying a Career Patterns approach to examining job requirements and building work environments is not a replacement for strategic workforce planning.

The analytic tool presented here was developed with the recognition that agencies are at different stages in their strategic workforce planning efforts. Agencies may have already determined which positions are critical to the agency mission and which positions are hard-to-fill or have high turnover. For agencies that already do labor market research, the analytic tool helps affirm plans and serves as a communication vehicle with senior officials to support decision making. Such agencies will proceed quickly through the initial steps of using the tool and find it helpful primarily to link previously identified job requirements to Career Pattern Scenarios. For agencies in the beginning or middle stages of workforce planning, this analytic tool provides a solid foundation for developing a systematic and competitive hiring strategy.

For more information about workforce planning and its central place in overall strategic human capital management, refer to the Human Capital Assessment and Accountability Framework (HCAAF) and Workforce Planning topics in Section IV of this guide. Additionally, the HCAAF Resource Center is available at: http://www.opm.gov/hcaaf_resource_center/index.asp

This Tool Can Benefit Multiple Users

User	Use
Strategic workforce planning practitioners	• Identify Career Pattern Scenarios to target to meet workforce needs, both short-term and long-term. • Define effective strategies for attracting and retaining workers in the Career Pattern Scenarios identified. • Analyze collective job requirements to identify top priority actions.
Recruiting and staffing HR practitioners	• Identify scenarios to target to effectively meet specific job requirements. • Identify the features of the work environment to stress in recruitment information to attract workers in targeted Career Pattern Scenarios.
CHCOs responsible for policy and agency practice	• Develop the business case for changes to human capital policies and practices needed to attract and retain required talent.
Line managers seeking to address pressing hiring and retention needs	• Identify the Career Pattern Scenarios to target to meet hiring and retention needs. • Shape work environment to be more appealing to workers in the Career Pattern Scenarios identified. • Identify attractors, i.e., the features of the work environment to stress when recruiting workers in these Career Pattern Scenarios.

The Analytic Tool: Analysis Process

The Career Patterns Analytic Tool provides a three-step process to analyze job requirements, categorize those requirements into Career Pattern Scenarios, and identify the work environment features your agency can use to attract a broader range of potential applicants and employees. The Career Patterns Analysis Worksheet will help you record information and conduct the analysis.

The following diagram summarizes the analysis process this tool applies.

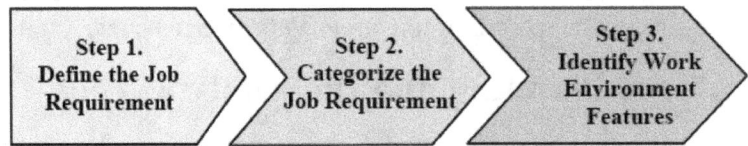

- **Step 1: Define the Job Requirement.** Identify and define your workforce requirements applying a broad set of criteria.

- **Step 2: Categorize the Job Requirement.** Answer a set of questions to translate your job requirements into Career Pattern Scenarios.

- **Step 3: Identify Work Environment Features**. Select work environment features your agency should support in order to attract and retain employees across a range of Career Patterns Scenarios. (The result of Step 3 will provide the basis for the Career Patterns Action Planning described in Section III.)

For agencies that have done some if not all of these steps already, this tool provides templates to capture existing observations and information systematically.

Step 1. Define the Job Requirement

Purpose: To understand and define the kinds of employees you want to hire and keep, both short-term and long-term.

Directions:

a. Define hiring and retention requirements on the Career Patterns Analysis Worksheet.
b. Enter each requirement on a separate row because requirements are best analyzed individually.
c. Define the nature and scope of the requirements. Consider defining your requirement using criteria such as:
   - Competencies
   - Occupational series
   - Range of work levels needed
   - Number of positions/employees needed
   - Geographic location
   - Timeframe

United States Office of Personnel Management

– CAREER PATTERNS ANALYSIS WORKSHEET –

Job Requirement (Step 1)	Career Pattern Scenarios (Step 2)	Work Environment Features (Step 3)		
		Feature	Current?	Future?
		[add additional rows as needed]		

STEP 1 TIPS:

- Break your requirement into smaller components if the nature of the job requirement is significantly different for geographic locations, organizational components, or other subsets of the overall requirement. For example, the requirement to hire program managers may call for a very different Career Pattern Scenario in a remote location than it would in larger metropolitan area.

- Define your job requirement in a way that doesn't reflect past preconceptions or otherwise presume a particular Career Pattern. For example, you should avoid describing your requirement as "entry-level engineers" because you may find upon further analysis that you could better meet your engineering talent needs by targeting Mid-Career Professionals rather than Students or New Professionals.

- Don't complete this step in a vacuum. Your strategic workforce plan should identify your short-term and long-term human capital needs. Make sure you align the job requirements you identify here with your strategic workforce plan. For example, you should be sure to account for workforce needs in all your mission critical occupations.

- It is not necessary to account for every vacancy or position. Instead, summarize or cluster specific job requirements into broader groupings that are similar in nature.

Case Study: the Agency for Health Care Administration (AHCA)

Throughout Sections II and III, we will use a case study to illustrate how to use the tool. The case describes some human capital issues the fictitious Agency for Health Care Administration (AHCA) is facing and how AHCA is using the Career Patterns approach to address them. After describing each step, we will show the result of how AHCA used the tool for that step.

Case Study: Human Capital in the Agency for Health Care Administration (AHCA)

AHCA, located in Washington, DC, has an aging workforce with over half its employees eligible for retirement within the next 5 years creating about 200 possible vacancies at all levels. The recent enactment of a new law places a new mandate on the agency that will require a significant increase in customer service and processing of electronic requests for the initial rollout of the program. The level of customer service is expected to decline after the initial roll-out and continue to decline for the next 3 years as customers enroll and gain a better understanding of the benefits program. AHCA's mission focuses heavily on providing a broad range of customer service.

AHCA has also determined a transformation of its information technology capabilities will contribute to more efficient and effective fulfillment of its mission. The agency currently has a limited information technology staff, but not the necessary personnel to lead the IT transformation effort. In addition to IT competence in the areas of computer programming and development, AHCA's requirements include personnel who can plan and execute robust enterprise architecture and can manage the organizational development challenge. There are 25 non-supervisory mid-level vacancies projected over the next 5 years

---

– Case Study – Step 1: AHCA Defines Job Requirements –

– CAREER PATTERNS ANALYSIS WORKSHEET –

Job Requirement (Step 1)	Career Pattern Scenarios (Step 2)	Work Environment Features (Step 3)		
		Feature	Current?	Future?
Customer Service and Health Insurance Requirement • 200 over the next 5 years • GS 5–12: multiple levels including supervisory and non-supervisory • Located in Washington, DC				
Information Technology Requirement • 5 per year for 5 years • GS 11–12: mid-level • Located in Washington, DC				

Step 2. Categorize Requirements into Career Pattern Scenarios

<u>Purpose</u>: To categorize your job requirements into one or more Career Pattern Scenarios.

The second step in the analytic process involves examining job requirements individually using a systematic method for assessing relevant work characteristics using the Career Patterns Analysis Questionnaire. By completing a questionnaire for each job requirement, you will identify Career Pattern Scenarios (i.e., groupings of workers) suited to and attracted by your job requirement. The relevant scenarios you identify will be recorded in the Career Patterns Analysis Worksheet.

This step relies heavily on the Career Patterns Analysis Questionnaire shown on page 37 and included in Appendix C. The questionnaire lists a comprehensive set of characteristics that can be used to describe and distinguish job requirements. These characteristics range among features such as the nature of the work to be performed, possibilities for using innovative work arrangements, various opportunities a job could offer for development, innovative work, applying new technologies, etc. No one job requirement will match all these characteristics.

The Career Patterns Analysis Questionnaire is designed to help you assess these characteristics for your particular job requirements to determine the Career Pattern Scenarios that may be most appropriate for your situation.

If none of the Career Pattern Scenarios adequately matches your requirements, you may want to define and build a new Career Pattern Scenario. To build a new scenario, refer to the information provided about the ten scenarios in Section I of this guide. Create this same kind of information for the tailored scenario you need.

> **STEP 2 TIPS**:
>
> – In assessing the characteristics in the Career Patterns Analysis Questionnaire for a particular job requirement, don't be constrained by what is or has been; think creatively about what could be possible in order to appeal to a broad range of potential applicants and employees.
>
> – When defining your requirements at Step 1, it may help to think first about the types of people you would want to hire to meet the requirement or who may already have the competencies you need. Then at Step 2 you can think about the Career Pattern Scenarios that best match the characteristics of those workers.

Directions for Step 2

a. Complete a separate Career Patterns Analysis Questionnaire for each of your job requirements. Enter a job requirement at the top of the first column to help keep track of the separate questionnaires.

b. For each requirement, review each characteristic in the first column of the questionnaire. If it applies to your job requirement, enter a check (✓) for that row in the second column.

c. After reviewing all the characteristics, highlight the rows you checked (✓).

d. At the bottom of each Career Pattern Scenario column, total the number of bullets in highlighted rows and compare that number with the total possible bullets for that scenario (shown in the row above).

e. Review those Career Pattern Scenarios where the job requirement's totals are closest to the columns' total possible bullets or where a substantial number of bullets were relevant. **These are the Career Patterns Scenarios you will want to consider.** You may also select other scenarios you believe would be appropriate for your job requirement irrespective of particular bullet totals. A rough rule of thumb is to select 2 to 5 scenarios at this stage.

f. Enter the names of all the selected scenarios from the Career Patterns Analysis Questionnaire onto the Career Patterns Analysis Worksheet under "Career Pattern Scenarios (Step 2)" in the worksheet row where you entered that job requirement in Step 1.

g. Think about whether the Career Pattern Scenarios you selected using the questionnaire and your judgment are likely to include workers who meet your needs from the perspective of your strategic human capital plan and your workforce plan. If a selected scenario would not fit your plans, strike that Career Pattern Scenario from those selected for that particular job requirement.

QUESTIONAIRE TIPS:

- The bullets in the cells of the questionnaire are predetermined, so they are already included in the questionnaire. The presence of a bullet in a cell indicates the Career Pattern Scenario named at the top of the column may be a logical target for meeting job requirements that have the characteristic for that row.

- You can create your own scenario! Adapt the template to add another column that fits the needs of your agency. You can insert bullets in the cells that correspond to characteristics that are relevant and make sense for your tailored scenario.

STEP 2
– CAREER PATTERNS ANALYSIS QUESTIONNAIRE –

Job Requirement (as defined at Step 1): [Insert your requirement here] — **This requirement …**	Check those that apply (✓)	Student	New Professional	Mid-Career Professional	Retiree	Highly Mobile	Revolving	Term	Mission-Focused	Experienced Professional	Requires Flexibilities
						Career Pattern Scenarios					
Provides opportunity to progress several grades as employees grow and learn		•	•								
Could be accomplished during non-standard work hours		•			•	•					•
Could be met through job sharing			•	•		•					
Allows employees flexibility to telework			•	•		•					•
Requires competencies and specialized skills that are unique to the agency		•	•		•					•	
Provides access to technology that is advanced for the profession or industry				•	•					•	
Involves work for which the labor market is highly competitive					•					•	•
Is governed by clear policies and procedures		•	•								
Calls for constant infusion of new ideas and ways of thinking							•	•			
Provides opportunity to interact or network with others in the industry or the profession				•	•						
Requires employees to be productive from day one, yet gives opportunity to progress by taking on more difficult assignments				•							
Requires people to come in and hit the ground running						•				•	
Provides opportunities to move from one geographic location to another several times over one's career						•					
Provides experiences that prepare employees who so desire to move to other agencies or to the private sector			•	•	•	•					
Is a temporary requirement that will end or change significantly in 1 to 2 years							•	•			
Is a temporary but recurring requirement that arises periodically							•				
Involves highly skilled duties at the cutting edge (e.g., opportunity to do world-class scientific research)				•						•	
Involves work that has a strong impact on important public missions									•		
Provides access to modern office technology such as remote and mobile network connectivity and internet applications		•	•			•					•
Involves close and regular interaction with others in a team environment		•	•		•				•		
Provides opportunities to develop new and advanced skills		•	•	•							
Provides visibility and recognition within the organization				•						•	
Is supported by a sound infrastructure of technical and logistical support				•			•	•		•	•
Provides a high level of independence and personal autonomy						•	•	•	•	•	•
Provides opportunities to make a significant impact on a humanitarian, economic, ecological or other cause									•		
Total possible bullets		7	9	10	7	8	5	4	4	8	6
Total bullets in checked (✓) rows											

– CAREER PATTERNS ANALYSIS QUESTIONNAIRE –

Job Requirement (as defined at Step 1): Customer Service and Health Insurance Requirement — This requirement …	Check those that Apply (✓)	Student	New Professional	Mid-Career Professional	Retiree	Highly Mobile	Revolving	Term	Mission-Focused	Experienced Professional	Requires Flexibilities
Provides opportunity to progress several grades as employees grow and learn	✓	•	•								
Could be accomplished during non-standard work hours		•			•	•					•
Could be met through job sharing	✓			•	•	•					
Allows employees flexibility to telework	✓		•	•	•	•					•
Requires competencies and specialized skills that are unique to the agency		•	•		•					•	
Provides access to technology that is advanced for the profession or industry			•	•						•	
Involves work for which the labor market is highly competitive	✓				•				•		•
Is governed by clear policies and procedures	✓	•	•								
Calls for constant infusion of new ideas and ways of thinking							•	•			
Provides opportunity to interact or network with others in the industry or the profession					•					•	
Requires employees to be productive from day one, yet gives opportunity to progress by taking on more difficult assignments	✓				•						
Requires people to come in and hit the ground running	✓				•					•	
Provides opportunities to move from one geographic location to another several times over one's career						•					
Provides experiences that prepare employees who so desire to move to other agencies or to the private sector	✓		•	•		•					
Is a temporary requirement that will end or change significantly in 1 to 2 years							•	•			
Is a temporary but recurring requirement that arises periodically							•				
Involves highly skilled duties at the cutting edge (e.g., opportunity to do world-class scientific research)					•					•	
Involves work that has a strong impact on important public missions									•		
Provides access to modern office technology such as remote and mobile network connectivity and internet applications		•	•			•					•
Involves close and regular interaction with others in a team environment	✓	•	•		•				•		
Provides opportunities to develop new and advanced skills	✓	•	•	•							
Provides visibility and recognition within the organization	✓			•						•	
Is supported by a sound infrastructure of technical and logistical support					•	•	•			•	•
Provides a high level of independence and personal autonomy						•	•	•		•	•
Provides opportunities to make a significant impact on a humanitarian, economic, ecological or other cause									•	•	
Total possible bullets		7	9	10	7	8	5	4	4	8	6
Total bullets in checked (✓) rows		4	6	6	5	3	0	0	2	2	2

NOTE: The blue areas identify the characteristics that apply to this job requirement (i.e., where row is checked (✓)). The yellow areas identify the Career Pattern Scenarios that may be closely associated with this job requirement.

– CAREER PATTERNS ANALYSIS QUESTIONNAIRE –

Job Requirement (as defined at Step 1): Information Technology Requirement — This requirement …	Check those that Apply (✓)	Career Pattern Scenarios									
		Student	New Professional	Mid-Career Professional	Retiree	Highly Mobile	Revolving	Term	Mission-Focused	Experienced Professional	Requires Flexibilities
Provides opportunity to progress several grades as employees grow and learn		•	•								
Could be accomplished during non-standard work hours	✓	•			•	•					•
Could be met through job sharing	✓		•	•	•	•					
Allows employees flexibility to telework	✓		•	•	•	•					•
Requires competencies and specialized skills that are unique to the agency		•	•	•						•	
Provides access to technology that is advanced for the profession or industry	✓		•	•						•	
Involves work for which the labor market is highly competitive	✓				•					•	•
Is governed by clear policies and procedures		•	•								
Calls for constant infusion of new ideas and ways of thinking							•	•			
Provides opportunity to interact or network with others in the industry or the profession					•					•	
Requires employees to be productive from day one, yet gives opportunity to progress by taking on more difficult assignments	✓			•							
Requires people to come in and hit the ground running					•					•	
Provides opportunities to move from one geographic location to another several times over one's career						•					
Provides experiences that prepare employees who so desire to move to other agencies or to the private sector	✓			•		•					
Is a temporary requirement that will end or change significantly in 1 to 2 years	✓						•	•			
Is a temporary but recurring requirement that arises periodically							•				
Involves highly skilled duties at the cutting edge e.g., opportunity to do world-class scientific research)					•					•	
Involves work that has a strong impact on important public missions									•		
Provides access to modern office technology such as remote and mobile network connectivity and internet applications	✓	•	•			•					•
Involves close and regular interaction with others in a team environment		•	•	•					•		
Provides opportunities to develop new and advanced skills	✓	•	•	•							
Provides visibility and recognition within the organization	✓			•						•	
Is supported by a sound infrastructure of technical and logistical support	✓			•		•			•		•
Provides a high level of independence and personal autonomy						•	•	•	•	•	•
Provides opportunities to make a significant impact on a humanitarian, economic, ecological or other cause							•	•			
Total possible bullets		7	9	10	7	8	5	4	4	8	6
Total bullets in checked (✓) rows		3	5	8	4	6	1	1	1	3	5

Note: The blue areas identify the characteristics that apply to this job requirement (i.e., where row is checked (✓)). The yellow areas identify the Career Pattern Scenarios that may be closely associated with this job requirement.

– Case Study – Step 2: AHCA Fills in Worksheet Column 2 with Selected Scenarios –

– CAREER PATTERNS ANALYSIS WORKSHEET –

Job Requirement	Career Pattern	Work Environment Features (Step 3)		
		Feature	Current?	Future?
Customer Service and Health Insurance Requirement • 200 over the next 5 years • GS 5 -12: multiple levels including supervisory and non-supervisory • Located in Washington, DC	• ~~Student~~* • New Professional • Mid-Career • Retiree			
Information Technology Requirement • 5 per year for 5 years • GS 11-12: mid-level • Located in Washington, DC	• Mid-Career Professional • Highly Mobile • Requires Flexibilities			

Note: After filling in the Career Pattern Scenarios suggested by the Career Patterns Analysis Questionnaire, AHCA decided it does not have the budget for outreach programs to students. Thus, the Student scenario will not be a focus of current planning.

Step 3. Identify Environment Features

Purpose: To identify the work environment features needed to appeal to workers in your selected Career Pattern Scenarios.

Directions:

a. Turn to Section I of this guide and review the Career Pattern Scenario(s) you selected in Step 2. Pay particular attention to the sections labeled "Work Attractors."

b. Identify those work attractors you think are most critical to appeal to the workers you are seeking for each of your job requirements. You may also identify other features of the work environment you think are critical to attract and retain the talent you need. Enter the attractors and other features you identify in the Career Patterns Analysis Worksheet under the column labeled "Work Environment Features."

c. After you identify relevant features, determine if that feature currently exists in your work environment or whether a policy, process, or practice would need to be changed in order for that feature to be present in your work environment. If the feature currently exists, check the column labeled "Current"; if the feature doesn't currently exist, check the column labeled "Future."

d. After completing the column labeled "Work Environment Features" on your Career Patterns Analysis Worksheet for all your job requirements, go back and identify those "Future" features of your work environment you believe are critical. You may want to focus on those that seem to appear again and again for multiple requirements; also consider any features you believe are important in order to meet your mission critical requirements.

e. Circle those "Future" features that you think are the top priorities your agency needs to focus on in making changes to policy, process, or practice. Also circle "Current" features where action is needed to promote or enhance the feature.

Once you have completed step 3, refer to Section III of this Guide for information on how to plan concrete actions to shape your work environment so it offers the features you identified.

> **STEP 3 TIPS**:
>
> –   Review your check marks on the Career Patterns Analysis Questionnaire. Where a characteristic is not checked, but it would appeal to the Career Pattern Scenarios you are targeting, consider what changes you would need to make to your work environment in order to make the characteristic apply in your agency. You may want to capture these changes on your Career Patterns Analysis Worksheet.

– Case Study – Step 3: AHCA notes desired work environment features as "Current" or "Future" –

– CAREER PATTERNS ANALYSIS WORKSHEET –

Requirement	Career Pattern (Step 2)	Work Environment Features (Step 3)			
		Feature		Current?	Future?
Customer Service and Health Insurance Requirement • 200 over the next 5 years • GS 5 -12: multiple levels including supervisory and non-supervisory • Located in Washington, DC	• ~~Student~~ • New Professional • Mid-Career • Retiree	1. Flexible work schedule and leave		1. ✔	1.
		2. Fair Compensation		2. ✔	2.
		3. Camaraderie		3. ✔	3.
		4. Advanced technology		4. ✔	4.
		5. Recognition		5.	5. ✔
		6. Innovative/meaningful work		6.	6. ✔
		7. Teamwork		7. ✔	7.
Information Technology Requirement • 5 per year for 5 years • GS 11-12: mid-level • Located in Washington, DC	• Mid-Career Professional • Highly Mobile • Requires Flexibilities	1. Flexible work schedule and leave		1.	1. ✔
		2. Fair Compensation		2. ✔	2.
		3. Advanced technology		3. ✔	3.
		4. Recognition		4.	4. ✔
		5. Innovative/meaningful work		5. ✔	5.
		6. Developmental opportunities		6.	6. ✔
		7. Flexible health benefits		7. ✔	7.
		8. Goal oriented projects		8.	8. ✔
		9. Networking opportunities		9.	9. ✔
		10. Retirement benefits		10. ✔	10.
		11. Technical, administrative, and logistical support		11. ✔	11.
		12. Benefits portability		12. ✔	12.
		13. Work aligned with interests		13. ✔	13.

III. Building Work Environments

This section uses the results of applying the Career Patterns Analytic Tool presented in Section II. It provides guidance to help you develop an action plan for building a work environment with the features needed to attract and retain a 21st century workforce. It also helps identify key messages about your work environment that you need to communicate to current and potential workers.

Prepare a Career Patterns Action Plan

Review the features you listed under "Work Environment Features" in your Career Patterns Analysis Worksheet (see Section II of this guide). This list identifies attractors that appeal to people in the Career Pattern Scenarios you selected for your agency. Identify which features currently exist at your agency and which features appear repeatedly in the list but are not a part of the current work environment.

For those features you circled as agency priorities on the Career Patterns Analysis Worksheet, identify the specific actions that must be taken to make the desired change or to effectively promote positive features to potential applicants and current employees. Also identify specific actions to educate managers and supervisors to be effective and successful in the new work environments. For each action, indicate who is responsible for taking action and when the action should be completed.

The intended end result is a work environment that appeals to the Career Pattern Scenarios you have targeted.

ACTION PLAN TIPS:

- Don't try to draw a one-for-one connection between every feature you listed under "Work Environment Features" in your Career Patterns Analysis Worksheet and the actions you list in your Career Patterns Action Plan. Many actions could address multiple features identified at Step 3 in Section II. Try to identify the actions that will have the biggest impact on the features you identified as important.

- After developing your action plan, make sure you incorporate critical goals and actions into your agency's strategic workforce plan.

Career Patterns Action Plan Template

Use a template at least as comprehensive as the following to record your action plan. You may also want to use a standard project planning tool to manage the actions you identify to shape your work environment.

– CAREER PATTERNS ACTION PLAN –

Action	Who	When

– Case Study – AHCA Develops a Career Patterns Action Plan –

Using the results of applying the Career Pattern Analysis Tool described in Section II of this guide, AHCA identified a number of features needed or currently present in its work environment that were important to attract and retain workers for its job requirements.

AHCA then reviewed these features and identified the actions it needed to accomplish in order to shape its work environment to appeal to current and potential workers. Those actions are listed in an Action Plan, along with the work environment features each action is intended to support. These features refer back to those listed on the Career Pattern Analysis Worksheet in Section II. It is important to note that all features listed on the worksheet do not necessarily need to be accounted for on the Action Plan. The intent is to identify practical actions that address those top priority features for AHCA or for a critical job requirement.

Action	Who	When
Restructure IT jobs to create opportunities to work on special projects; restructure Customer Service and Health Insurance Specialist jobs to break up routine tasks with tasks to investigate and solve problems and improve processes. Supports these features: Goal-oriented projects, Work that's innovative/meaningful	HR – work with managers to identify and assess restructuring opportunities	12/06
Partner with professional groups to encourage and facilitate participation of IT Specialists in professional association activities and certification programs. Supports these features : Networking opportunities	Designated IT Office Manager	10/06
Review network security policies to allow remote network access needed to perform work activities from home. Supports these features: Flexible work schedules and leave	Network Security Manager	9/06
Define career paths for movement to higher level positions and provide guidance on training and development resources needed to progress through the career paths. Supports these features: Development opportunities	HR – lead role, working in partnership with management team	2/07
Establish an on-the-spot awards program to provide regular recognition for employee accomplishments. Supports these features: Recognition	HR – lead role, working in partnership with management team	12/06
Develop standardized supporting text for inclusion in vacancy announcements and recruiting materials that clearly articulates flexible benefits, retirement benefits, benefits portability, fair compensation, work schedule and leave flexibilities offered by the Agency, as well as the team environment in which work is done and camaraderie among staff. Supports these features: Flexible benefits, Retirement benefits, Benefits portability, Fair compensation, Flexible work schedules and leave, Teamwork, and Camaraderie.	HR	9/06

United States Office of Personnel Management

IV. Resources and Tools

This Section identifies resources and tools for hiring managers, HR practitioners and employees that can help them operate effectively using the Career Patterns approach environment. The following table will guide you to specific resources and tools based upon the actions you identified earlier.

If your Career Patterns Action Plan includes …	You may want to explore …
Promote Unique Aspects Of Working At Your Agency	Writing Effective Vacancy Notices
Promulgate Employment Information	USAJOBS and Studentjobs.gov
Launch Telework Initiative	Telework Resources
Expand Intern Program	Studentjobs.gov Flexibilities and Authorities
Promote US Government's Benefits Package/TSP	Writing Effective Vacancy Notices Flexibilities and Authorities
Market Flexibilities for Students	Flexibilities and Authorities
Offer Recruitment Incentives/Tuition Reimbursement	Flexibilities and Authorities
Open Vacancies To Competition From External Applicants	Writing Effective Vacancy Notices Flexibilities and Authorities
Create Part-Time and Flexible Work Options	Workforce Planning Flexibilities and Authorities
Develop Recruiting Outreach Programs	Workforce Planning Flexibilities and Authorities

THE HCAAF RESOURCE CENTER

The Human Capital Assessment and Accountability Framework (HCAAF) Resource Center is a comprehensive collection of strategies, tools, and methods for agencies to use as they plan, implement, and evaluate strategic human capital management. The Resource Center provides an electronic Practitioners Guide based on the HCAAF, a road map for human capital transformation. The HCAAF evolved from a set of Human Capital standards, issued by the Office of Personnel Management (OPM) in 2002, which were developed through a collaborative effort among OPM, the Office of Management and Budget (OMB), and the Government Accountability Office (GAO). The HCAAF establishes and defines five human capital systems that together provide a single, consistent definition of human capital management for the Federal Government. The Resource Center is found at http://www.opm.gov/hcaaf_resource_center/.

The HCAAF Resource Center and its embedded Practitioners Guide is intended to accelerate Governmentwide efforts to support agency mission results with strong human capital strategies. When used as a comprehensive standard for human capital results, human resources (HR) programs, and merit system compliance, the Guide serves as the basis for agency strategic human capital management accountability systems that meet OPM requirements.

The HCAAF's Talent Management System provides comprehensive information about how to address the gaps and deficiencies in the skills, knowledge, and competencies of employees in mission-critical occupations in the current and future workforces. The agency's strategic human capital plan – and its workforce plans – drive recruitment activities that are encompassed in the Career Patterns approach.

Workforce Planning

To make the Federal Government competitive for the best talent America has to offer, the hiring process needs to be lean, fast, and effective. To be ready to hire swiftly, agencies must do their "strategic homework" by conducting workforce planning, an important part of the Strategic Alignment System, the planning and goal setting system of the HCAAF.

The results that agencies are expected to achieve through workforce planning may be found in the HCAAF Resource Center at http://www.opm.gov/hcaaf_resource_center/3-4.asp. This site also contains detailed information about the key elements of a workforce plan and suggested effectiveness and compliance indicators to help determine the adequacy of the agency's workforce plan. Through workforce planning, agencies are able to:

- Identify and document mission-critical occupations and competencies
- Identify competency gaps between the current and future workforce
- Identify gap reduction strategies, i.e., make decisions about structuring and deploying the workforce to best support the agency mission.

OPM's Website for Strategic Management of Human Capital contains a workforce planning model (https://www.opm.gov/hcaaf_resource_center/assets/Sa_tool4.pdf) to guide agencies on how to develop and implement successful workforce plans. This tool should be used in conjunction with the workforce planning guidance contained in the HCAAF Resource Center (http://www.opm.gov/hcaaf_resource_center/3-4.asp). The site also includes best practices on workforce analysis planning measures agencies have completed and provides examples, resources and links to successful workforce planning initiatives (https://www.opm.gov/egov/documents/MPG/MPG2_Information_Workforce_Planning_Best%20Practicesv2.pdf).

USAJOBS and Studentjobs.gov

USAJOBS is the Federal government's centralized one-stop shopping service for agency vacancy announcements and various items of relevant employment information available 24/7. USAJOBS is accessible through two delivery systems in which vacancy announcements and employment information are available to all customers-job seekers, Federal employees, and the general public:

- Website at http://www.usajobs.gov/
- USAJOBS Interactive Voice Response system at 703-724-1850 (978-461-8404 TDD)

USAJOBS offers a variety of features to support recruiting efforts of Federal agencies:

- A wide array of job searches allows applicants to search jobs by location, agency, series and keywords.
- Employment fact sheets provide information on a wide variety of topics related to Federal employment issues, including agency-specific fact sheets.
- USAJOBS by Email features a capability for job seekers to specify up to ten customized job searches and then receive automatic emails when new jobs are posted that match those search criteria. The emails provide links directly to the vacancy announcements.
- Agency search pages can be created for any agency to advertise either internal and/or external positions.
- Hot Jobs, Featured Jobs and Featured Employer areas allow agencies to post jobs that are critical or hard to fill.
- Banner ads can help agencies highlight their special hiring needs.
- A resume builder feature allows individuals to create up to five resumes. Job seekers can choose to make their resumes "searchable" and thus increase their opportunities of being invited to apply for hard-to-fill positions by Federal agencies conducting resume mining.
- Studentjobs.gov (http://www.studentjobs.gov/) provides a one-stop shopping service that is strictly for student and e-Scholar opportunities within the Federal government.

Writing Effective Vacancy Notices

Under continuing efforts to modernize and streamline the hiring process, OPM encourages agencies to use the five-tabbed job announcement format and accept job applications and resumes online. The hiring makeover project included a guide to writing effective vacancies (https://www.opm.gov/hiringtoolkit/docs/job_posting_template-generic_12_06_05.pdf) using USAJOBS' five-tabbed job announcement format. The template includes instructions, key requirements, and examples for each tab area.

Flexibilities and Authorities

OPM has designed a handbook, Human Resources Flexibilities and Authorities in the Federal Government that examines human resources (HR) flexibilities and authorities and how they can be used to manage your human capital challenges. This handbook is divided into three major parts: Part I describes the foundation of our Government-wide human resource system as a "single employer" and highlights the common policies that make for good public policy. Part II is designed for the General Schedule system and Federal Wage System, and Part III is for the Senior Executive Service.

A list of high-impact HR flexibilities is included in this guide as Appendix A.

OPM has also designed a Website, Federal Hiring Flexibilities Resource Center (http://www.opm.gov/Strategic_Management_of_Human_Capital/fhfrc/default.asp) that includes strategies and tools to assist you in exploring various hiring flexibilities. The Website will also help you match potential hiring flexibilities with your needs.

Competitive Examining Process
OPM's comprehensive Delegated Examining Operations Handbook (https://www.opm.gov/deu/Handbook_2007/DEO_Handbook.pdf) provides a flow chart for the Competitive Examining Process.

Telework Resources

Interagency Telework Website (http://www.telework.gov/)
The Office of Personnel Management (OPM) and the General Services Administration (GSA) have established a joint Web site on Telework to provide access to guidance issued by both agencies. Here you will find information for employees who think they might like to telecommute (or are already doing so), for managers and supervisors who supervise teleworkers, and for agency telework coordinators.

Resources for Supervisors
The Interagency telework site contains information to help people who supervise teleworkers, or are going to need to do so. Here are the links to some of the most popular helpful resources you'll find at the website:

- Basics for Managers (http://www.telework.gov/Tools_and_Resources/Basics_Managers/index.aspx)
- Telework 101 for Managers (http://www.telework.gov/tools_and_resources/training/managers/index.aspx)
- Frequently Asked Questions (http://www.telework.gov/faq/Manager/index.aspx)

United States Office of Personnel Management

V. Appendices

Appendix A: High Impact HR Flexibilities

<u>Flexible Pay</u>

- **Recruitment and Relocation Incentives:** Recruitment and relocation incentives are discretionary payments agencies may use to provide additional compensation (generally up to 25 percent of the annual rate of basic pay times the number of years in the service agreement, not to exceed four years) to a new appointee or to an employee who moves to a different geographic area. An agency must make a determination that a position would be difficult to fill in the absence of an incentive.

- **Retention Incentives:** Retention incentives are discretionary payments agencies may use to provide additional compensation (generally up to 25 percent of basic pay) when the unusually high or unique qualifications of an employee or a special need of the agency for the employee's services makes it essential to retain the employee and the agency determines the employee is likely to leave Federal service in the absence of an incentive.

- **Superior Qualifications And Special Needs Pay-Setting Authority (also known as "above minimum hiring rate"):** Agencies may set the rate of basic pay of a newly-appointed employee at a rate above the minimum rate of the appropriate General Schedule (GS) grade because of (1) the superior qualifications of the candidate, or (2) a special need of the agency for the candidate's services.

- **Maximum Payable Rate Rule (highest previous rate):** Upon reemployment, transfer, reassignment, promotion, demotion, or change in type of appointment, agencies may set the rate of basic pay of an employee by taking into account a rate of basic pay previously received by the individual while employed in another civilian Federal position (with certain exceptions). This rate may not exceed the maximum rate of the employee's grade.

<u>Flexible Hiring</u>

- **Dual Comp Waivers** (*may require modification*): Agencies may request OPM to waive dual compensation restrictions for civilian and military retirees, on a case-by-case basis, for employees in positions for which there is exceptional difficulty in recruiting or retaining a qualified employee, or to meet an emergency hiring need as specified in law. (5 U.S.C. 8344 and 8468; 5 CFR part 553, subpart B)

- **Temporary Limited Appointment NTE 1-year:** Use temporary appointments for short-term needs that are not expected to last longer than one year.

- **Term Appointment for 1-4 years:** Use term appointments for more than one and up to four years when the need for the employee's services is not permanent for needs such as project work, extraordinary workload, etc.

- **Excepted Appointing Authorities**: OPM provides excepted service hiring authorities to fill special jobs or to fill any job in unusual or special circumstances under "Schedules A, B, and C." These excepted service authorities enable agencies to hire when it is not feasible or not practical to use traditional competitive hiring procedures, and can streamline hiring.

    - **Federal Career Intern Program**: This program helps agencies recruit and attract exceptional individuals into a variety of occupations. It was created under Executive Order 13162 and is for positions at grade levels GS-5, 7, and 9 or other trainee positions. In general, individuals are appointed to a 2-year internship. Upon successful completion of the internships, the interns may be eligible for permanent placement within an agency.

    - **Presidential Management Fellows (PMF) Program**: The Presidential Management Intern Program, a predecessor to this program, was established by Executive Order in 1977. The PMF program attracts to the Federal service outstanding graduate students (masters and doctoral-level) from a wide variety of academic disciplines who have an interest in, and commitment to, a career in the analysis and management of public policies and programs.

    - **Senior Presidential Management Fellow or Senior Fellow:** This program is used to appoint individuals at the GS-13, GS-14, or GS-15 level (or equivalent) in the excepted service or under an agency-specific authority if the agency is excepted from the competitive service. The individual must have completed a graduate course of study at a qualifying college or university; have an outstanding record of achievement in an applicable leadership, policy, managerial, professional, or technical position or area; have successfully completed an OPM-administered assessment process; been selected as a finalist by the OPM Director, or the Director's designee; and been appointed by an agency as a Senior Fellow. (This program has not yet been put into operation).

    - **Student Career Experience Program (SCEP):** This is a special authority under which agencies can appoint students who are enrolled or have been accepted for enrollment in at least a part-time schedule at an accredited institution. Individuals in the SCEP program may be non-competitively converted to term or career/career-conditional appointments within 120 days of academic requirement completion. Students hired under SCEP may be granted tuition assistance by the hiring agency.

    - **Student Temporary Employment Program (STEP)**: This program provides authority to appoint graduate and undergraduate students in the excepted service under the Student Educational Employment Program. This is a special authority under which agencies can appoint students who are enrolled or have been accepted for enrollment in at least a part-time schedule at an accredited institution. Appointment in the STEP program is not to exceed one year and may not be converted to term or permanent.

- **Veterans Appointing Authorities:** Veterans may be hired into the Federal Government in a variety of ways including the following three authorities: Veterans Recruitment Appointment (VRA), 30 Percent or More Disabled Veterans, and the Veterans Employment Opportunities Act of 1998 (VEOA).

- **Appointment of Experts and Consultants:** This excepted service appointment is used to hire expert and consultants under 5 U.S.C. 3109 to perform expert or consultant work that is temporary (not to exceed one year) or intermittent.

- **Direct-Hire Authority**: This authority allows agencies with delegated examining authority to hire individuals without regard to sections 3309-3318 of title 5 to positions for which:
  - Public notice has been given, *and*
  - The U.S. Office of Personnel Management determines there is a *severe shortage* of candidates or a *critical hiring* need.

- **Reinstatement Eligibility:** Reinstatement allows a former civil service employee to reenter the Federal competitive service workforce without competing with the public in a civil service examination but only after meeting certain requirements.

- **Intergovernmental Personnel Act (IPA) Mobility Program**: This program is used to bring in temporary assignees from state and local governments, colleges and universities, Indian tribal governments, and other not-for-profit organizations under the Intergovernmental Personnel Act (IPA) Mobility Program. Assignments should be made for the mutual benefit of the Federal Government and the non-Federal entity, and are for 2 years duration.

Flexible Work Arrangements

- **Flexible Work Schedules and Leave Policies**: Flexible work schedules and compressed work schedules (commonly known as "alternative work schedules") allow an employee to complete the basic 80-hour biweekly work requirement in less than 10 workdays. Flexible leave programs and policies provide employees generous amounts of paid leave for personal needs, medical needs, family care, and vacations.

- **Part-time and/or Job Sharing**: Making appointments with varying work schedules such as part-time (which may include job sharing arrangements), intermittent, and seasonal is a viable option to manage fluctuating and less than full-time workforce needs. Job sharing is an available option that may help balance some employees' work and family responsibilities. Under such an arrangement, two employees each work less than full-time, but coordinate their schedules and assignments so that together they "share" a work role and ensure that the duties and responsibilities of what would otherwise be one full-time position are properly carried out.

- **Telework:** Telework refers to any arrangement in which an employee performs officially assigned duties at home or other worksites geographically convenient to the residence of the employee. Telework.gov is a comprehensive Website co-sponsored by the General Services Administration and OPM. It includes the latest guidance, assistance and resources, and agency telework policies to review.

Flexible Benefits

- **Flexible Spending Accounts**: There are two types of FSAs. A Health Care FSA (HCFSA) pays for the uncovered or unreimbursed portions of qualified medical costs. A Dependent Care FSA (DCFSA) allows you to pay eligible expenses for dependent care with pre-tax dollars. All employee contributions to FSAs are made from pre-tax earnings, thereby increasing disposable income. There are no government contributions to the FSAFEDS program and you have to enroll anew each open season.

- **Student Loan Repayment Program:** Using this authority, agencies may repay Federally insured student loans as a recruitment or retention incentive for appointees or current employees. Agencies may make payments to the loan holder of up to a maximum of $10,000 for an employee in a calendar year and a total of not more than $60,000 for any one employee.

- **Tuition Reimbursement**: Agencies may offer employees financial assistance to attend academic courses that are job related.

- **Childcare and Eldercare Benefits**: The government offers a variety of these benefits, some of which may vary by agency and location. They include On-site/Near-site Child Development Centers, Child Care Subsidy Authority, Dependent Care Spending Accounts, and Other Child and Elder Care Services.

- **Thrift Savings Plan Matching:** Employees covered by the Federal Employees' Retirement System are eligible to receive: 1) Agency Automatic (1%) Contributions; 2) Agency Matching Contributions of up to 4% of basic pay; 3) Immediate vesting in Agency Matching Contributions and vesting – generally in 3 years – in Agency Automatic (1%) Contributions. Civil Service Retirement System participants do not receive any agency contributions.

- **Benefits for Temporary Limited, Term, and Other Than Full-time Career Employment:** Benefits vary according to the type of appointment made.

– High Impact HR Flexibilities Mapped to Career Pattern Scenarios –

Flexibility or Authority	HR Flexibilities and Authorities Handbook*	Student	New Professional	Mid-Career	Retiree	Highly Mobile	Revolving	Term	Mission-Focused	Experienced Professional	Requires Flexibilities
Pay											
Recruitment or Relocation Incentives[1]	E-1&2		H	H	M	H	H		H	H	
Superior Quals & Special Needs Pay-Setting Auth.	E-4		M	H	H	H	H	H	H	H	
Maximum Payable Rate Rule[2]	E-5				H		M		H	H	
Dual Comp Waivers	E-6				H						
Hiring											
Temporary Appointment	A-3						M				
Term Appointment	A-3		H				H	H			
Excepted Appointing Authorities[3]	A-4	H	H	H						M	
Veterans Appointing Authorities	A-4	H	M	M		M			H	M	
Appointment of Experts and Consultants	A-4			H	H	M	H		H		
Direct-Hire Authority	A-4		M	M				M	H		
Reinstatement Eligibility	A-4				H	H	H	M			
Intergov'tal Personnel Act (IPA) Mobility Program	J-3			M		H	H	H			
Work Arrangements											
Flexible Work Schedules and Leave Policies	C-1&3	H	H	H	H	H	H	H	H	H	H
Part-Time and/or Job Sharing	A-4	H		M	H						H
Telework	C-2	H	H	H	H	H	H	H	H	H	H
Benefits											
Flexible Spending Accounts	D-7		M	M		M	M	M	M	M	M
Student Loan Repayment Program	E-11	M	H			M			H		
Tuition Reimbursement	J-1	H	H					M	M		
Childcare and Eldercare Benefits	C-6		M	H	M					M	H
Thrift Savings Plan (TSP) Matching	D-5		H	H	H	H	H	H	H	H	H
Part-Time/Term Benefits	Many	H			H		H				H

* For more information, turn to the indicated section of Part II in the HR Flexibilities and Authorities Handbook.

"H" indicates the flexibility is **H**ighly effective in attracting candidates from the given scenario; "M" indicates **M**oderately effective.

[1] Relocation is only for current employees. Recruitment is only for those who are not current employees.

[2] Rule uses rate earned in a previous Federal civilian position.

[3] For Student: FCIP, PMF, STEP, SCEP. For New Professional: FCIP, PMF, SCEP. For Mid-Career SPMF. For Exp'd Prof: SPMF.

FCIP - Federal Career Intern Program

PMF - Presidential Management Fellow

STEP - Student Temporary Employment Program

SCEP - Student Career Experience Program

SPMF - Senior Presidential Management Fellow

Appendix B: Bibliography

A rich body of human capital research underpins the Career Patterns initiative. These articles are among those reviewed in developing the Career Patterns concepts.

1. "2003 Spherion® Emerging Workforce® Study," Spherion Pacific Enterprises LLC, 2002-2003.

2. "A New Call to Service for an Age of Savvy Altruism: Public Attitudes about Government and Government Workers," Partnership for Public Service, August 2004.

3. "A Systems Approach: Maximizing Individual Career Potential and Organizational Success," Linda M. Kutilek, Gail J. Gunderson, Nikki L. Conklin, Journal of Extension, April 2002.

4. "A Work Experience Second to None: Impelling the Best to Serve," National Academy of Public Administration, September 2001.

5. "Acceptance of Telework Expands Labor Pool," Rebecca R. Hastings, Society for Human Resource Management, February 2006.

6. "Age Wave: Adapting to Older Workers," Workforce Management, March 2006.

7. "Aging, Adult Development, And Work Motivation," Ruth Kanfer, Phillip L. Ackerman, Academy Of Management Review, 2004.

8. "An Employer's Guide to Older Workers: How to Win Them Back and Convince Them to Stay," Barbara McIntosh, Ph.D., U.S. Department of Labor, 2001.

9. "Asking the Wrong Questions: A Look at How the Federal Government Assesses and Selects Its Workforce," Partnership for Public Service, October 2004.

10. "Attracting and Keeping The Best and the Brightest: Survey Results From Council for Excellence in Government Principals on How to Get, Develop and Retain Excellent People in Government Service," Council for Excellence in Government, 2002.

11. "Attracting and Retaining the Mature Workforce," Barbara McIntosh, Ph.D., Society for Human Resource Management, November 2005.

12. "Building an Employment "Brand – A Compilation of Articles," Dr John Sullivan, Employment Branding Whitepaper, 2004.

13. "Building and Boosting the Employer Brand," Carla Joinson, Society For Human Resource Management, Summer 2002.

14. "Career Development of Free Agent Workers," Susan Imel, ERIC Clearinghouse on Adult Career and Vocational Education, 2001.

15. "Career Development of Older Adults," Susan Imel, ERIC Clearinghouse on Adult Career and Vocational Education, 2001.

16. "Creativity Is Key to Meeting Multigenerational Workforce Needs," Theresa Minton-Eversole, Society for Human Resource Management, 2005.

17. "Employee Engagement Report," BlessingWhite, Inc., 2005.

18. "Employers Exploring Ways To Retain Older Workers," Pamela Babcock, October 2005.

19. "Finding the Civil Service's Hidden Sex Appeal: Why The Brightest Young People Shy Away From Government," Nicholas Thompson, The Washington Monthly, November 2000

20. "Flexible Work Arrangements: The Demand Will Only Strengthen," Donna J. Bear, Human Resource Institute, September 2004.

21. "Generational Differences: Survey Report," Society for Human Resource Management, August 2004.

22. "Generations at Work" Human Resource Institute, Judy London, June 2005.

23. "Graying of Society: Increasing Life Spans and Low Fertility Rates Are Combining to Create Population Imbalance," Judy London, Human Resource Institute-HRI, March 2004.

24. "How To Attract Scientists," Celia M. Henry, Employment, October 2001.

25. "Business Case for Workers 50+: Planning for Tomorrow's Talent Needs in Today's Competitive Environment," A Report for AARP Prepared by Towers Perrin, December 2005.

26. "Increasing the Odds of Success with Outside Experienced Hires: A Case Study of Competency-based Assessment and Selection," Hay Group, 2003.

27. "Insights on the Federal Government's Human Capital Crisis: Reflections of Generation X," Amit Bordia and Tony Cheesebrough, Partnership for Public Service, 2002.

28. "Job Compensation/Pay Survey Report'" Society for Human Resource Management/CNNfn, Evren Esen, January 2004.

29. "Job Satisfaction Survey Report 2004," Evren Esen, Society for Human Resource Management, April 2004.

30. "Leadership Styles: Generational Differences," Nancy R. Lockwood, SPHR, GPHR, HR Content Expert, Society for Human Resource Management, 2004.

31. "Leadership: The Key Factor in HR Strategic Management," Nancy R. Lockwood, SPHR, GPHR, HR Content Expert, Society for Human Resource Management, December 2004.

32. "Mid-Career Hiring In The Federal Government: A Strategy For Change," The Partnership for Public Service, February 2002.

33. "Mid-Career Hiring: Revisiting the Search for Seasoned Talent in the Federal Government," Partnership for Public Service, September 2004.

34. "PRB Reports on America: The Career Quandary," Phyllis Moen, Population Reference Bureau, February 2001.

35. "Public Opinion on Public Service," Partnership for Public Service, May 2005.

36. "Putting Aging Workforce on Employment Planning Radar: Results from an AARP/Florida Trend Survey," Rachelle Cummins, AARP, October 2005.

37. "Retention, Engagement Highest Among Companies with Most Effective Communication Strategies," Theresa Minton-Eversole, Society for Human Resource Management, February 2006.

38. SHRM Human Capital Benchmarking Study," Society for Human Resource Management 2005.

39. "Six Ways to Mine Teen Talent," Andrea C. Poe, Society for Human Resource Management, March 2001.

40. "Staying Ahead of the Curve 2004: Employer Best Practices for Mature Workers," Study Conducted for AARP by Mercer Human Resource Consulting, September 2004.

41. "Strategies for Recruiting Workers Over Age 50," Society for Human Resource Management, Cathy Fyock, December 2005.

42. "Taking Action Against the Quiet Crisis in Recruitment and Retention," AFT Public Employees, AFL-CIO.

43. "Talent Management: Employee Engagement: Talent Management Series Part III," Nancy R. Lockwood, SPHR, GPHR, Society for Human Resource Management, July 2005.

44. "Talent Management: Leadership Development: Talent Management Series Part II," Nancy R. Lockwood, SPHR, GPHR, Society for Human Resource Management, July 2005.

45. "Talent Management: Overview: Talent Management Series Part I," Nancy R. Lockwood, SPHR, GPHR, Society for Human Resource Management, July 2005.

46. "Talent Management," Shawn Fegley and Nancy Lockwood, SPHR, GPHR, Society for Human Resource Management, January 2006.

47. "Tapping America's Potential: Expanding Student Employment and Internship Opportunities in the Federal Government," Partnership for Public Service, July 2002.

48. "Telework: Shifting Into Gear," CDW-G, March 2006.

49. "The Aging Workforce: The Reality of the Impact of Older Workers and Eldercare in the Workplace," Nancy R. Lockwood, Society for Human Resource Management, December 2003.

50. "The Blended Workforce: Maximizing Agility through Nonstandard Work Arrangements," IBM Center for the Business of Government, April 2005.

51. "The Business Case for Workers Age 50+: Planning for Tomorrow's Talent Needs," Towers Perrin, AARP, December 2005.

52. "The Capability Within: The Global Human Capital Study 2005," Randy McDonald and Mary Sue Rogers, IBM Business Consulting Services, 2005.

53. "The Chained Gang—Human Capital Management: The Human Capital Challenge," Mark A. Abramson, Ruby Butler Demesme, and Nicole Willenz Gardner, The Journal of Public Inquiry, Spring/Summer 2002.

54. "The Compelling Offer A Quantitative Analysis of the Career Preferences and Decisions of High Value Employees," Corporate Leadership Council, 1999.

55. "The Employment Brand: Building Competitive Advantage in the Labor Market," Corporate Leadership Council, 1999.

56. "The Quiet Crisis: Recruitment and Retention in the Public Sector," Federation of Public Employees/AFT.

57. "The Recruiting Challenge: What Do You Know About Older Workers?" Katherine L. Y. Green, Ph.D. and Andrea Hodson, SPHR, Society for Human Resource Management, October 2005.

58. "They Want You! - U.S. government has difficulty attracting high quality job candidates - Brief Article - Statistical Data Included," American Demographics, January 2002.

59. "Twenty-Something Job Candidates Expect Speed: Online Networks Help Recruiters Keep Up With Millennials," Mollie Ziegler, Federal Times, April 2006.

60. "Update On The Older Worker: 2004," AARP, April 2005.

61. "Using A Systems Approach to Maximize Human Potential or Individual and Organizational Success," Nikki L. Conklin and Linda M. Kutilek, AIAEE 2003 Proceedings of the 19th Annual Conference, 2003.

62. "Voluntary Employee Benefits Series Part I: Voluntary Benefits & Job Satisfaction," Leslie A. Weatherly, SPHR, HR Content Expert, Society for Human Resource Management, December 2005.

63. "Winning the Best and Brightest: Increasing the Attraction of Public Service," Carol Chetkovich, The PricewaterhouseCoopers Endowment for The Business of Government, July 2001.

64. "Women in the Workforce," Carol Morrison, Human Resource Institute, June 2005.

65. "Workplace Diversity: Leveraging the Power of Difference for Competitive Advantage," Nancy R. Lockwood, SPHR, GPHR, Society for Human Resource Management, April 2006.

Appendix C: Worksheet / Questionnaire

Blank templates for the Career Patterns Analysis Worksheet and the Career Patterns Analysis Questionnaire are provided on the following pages.

– CAREER PATTERNS ANALYSIS WORKSHEET –

Job Requirement (Step 1)	Career Pattern Scenarios (Step 2)	Work Environment Features (Step 3)		
		Feature	Current?	Future?
	[add additional rows as needed]			

STEP 2
– CAREER PATTERNS ANALYSIS QUESTIONNAIRE –

Instructions

- Complete this questionnaire separately for each job requirement you defined in step 1 of the analysis process.
- Review each characteristic; if it applies to your job requirement, enter a check (✔) for that row in the second column.
- After reviewing all characteristics, highlight the rows you checked (✔).
- At the bottom of each column, total the number of bullets in highlighted rows and compare that number with the total possible bullets for that scenario in the row above. These are the Career Pattern Scenarios you will want to consider. Select other scenarios you believe would be appropriate for your job requirement irrespective of bullet totals.
- Enter all selected scenarios in the Career Patterns Analysis Worksheet under "Career Pattern Scenarios."

Job Requirement (as defined at Step 1): [Insert your requirement here]	Check those that apply (✔)	Student	New Professional	Mid-Career Professional	Retiree	Highly Mobile	Revolving	Term	Mission-Focused	Experienced Professional	Requires Flexibilities
This requirement…											
Provides opportunity to progress several grades as employees grow and learn		•	•								
Could be accomplished during non-standard work hours		•			•	•					•
Could be met through job sharing				•	•	•					
Allows employees flexibility to telework			•	•	•	•					•
Requires competencies and specialized skills that are unique to the agency		•	•		•					•	
Provides access to technology that is advanced for the profession or industry			•	•						•	
Involves work for which the labor market is highly competitive						•			•		•
Is governed by clear policies and procedures		•	•								
Calls for constant infusion of new ideas and ways of thinking							•	•			
Provides opportunity to interact or network with others in the industry or the profession					•					•	
Requires employees to be productive from day one, yet gives opportunity to progress by taking on more difficult assignments					•						
Requires people to come in and hit the ground running						•				•	
Provides opportunities to move from one geographic location to another several times over one's career						•					
Provides experiences that prepare employees who so desire to move to other agencies or to the private sector			•	•		•					
Is a temporary requirement that will end or change significantly in 1 to 2 years							•	•			
Is a temporary but recurring requirement that arises periodically							•				
Involves highly skilled duties at the cutting edge (e.g., opportunity to do world-class scientific research)				•						•	
Involves work that has a strong impact on important public missions									•		
Provides access to modern office technology such as remote and mobile network connectivity and internet applications		•	•			•					•
Involves close and regular interaction with others in a team environment		•	•		•				•		
Provides opportunities to develop new and advanced skills		•	•	•							
Provides visibility and recognition within the organization				•						•	
Is supported by a sound infrastructure of technical and logistical support				•			•	•		•	•
Provides a high level of independence and personal autonomy							•	•	•	•	•
Provides opportunities to make a significant impact on a humanitarian, economic, ecological or other cause									•	•	
Total possible bullet points		7	9	10	7	8	5	4	4	8	6
Total bullet points in checked (✔) rows											